Praise for Red Zone Selling

"Red Zone Selling is the first sales playbook that actually feels like game day. Vince doesn't just teach you how to close, he shows you how to control the field, read the defense, and finish strong. Every chapter hits like a two-minute drill for enterprise deals."

— Justin Michael,
bestselling author, *Cold Call Algo*

"Red Zone Selling flips the script on traditional sales books. Vince gives you a clear framework to stay in control, create buyer value, and win when it counts. It's not just smart, it's built for sellers who want to close with confidence."

— Andy Paul,
author, *Sell Without Selling Out*

"Red Zone Selling is a high-impact playbook for enterprise sellers who are tired of losing deals in the final stretch. Vince Beese combines battle-tested tactics with sports metaphors that actually work, delivering a clear, actionable framework to qualify better, build real momentum, and close with precision. This isn't theory—it's a system designed by someone who's lived it."

— Scott Leese,
Founder, Sales Leader, Author, Speaker

"Red Zone Selling aligns perfectly with my approach: it's relentless in driving value, not just pushing deals, ensuring sellers win big by guiding customers toward real outcomes."

— Jamal Reimer,
founder of Whyzer.ai, and author of *Mega Deal Secrets*

"As a former college baseball player, I've seen how most games are won in the clutch ... essentially, the 'Red Zone' of pressure and performance. Red Zone Selling brings that same intensity to sales, as Vince Beese delivers a championship playbook that helps reps step up, call the right play, and close when it counts. Truly, a 'MUST-READ' for anyone ready to win big in sales."

— Larry Long Jr.,
Chief Energy Office of LLJR Enterprises,
4x Salesforce Top Sales Influencer

"This book nails it. Red Zone Selling is the closest thing to a field manual for enterprise reps who want to stop winging it and start closing like pros. Every chapter delivers tactical plays that actually work when the pressure is on."

— Dustin Brown,
Global Strategic SaaS Sales

"Red Zone Selling brings the clarity, precision, and discipline elite sales teams need to win. This isn't theory, it's a practical, execution-first framework that helps sellers qualify hard, build real momentum, and close with confidence. Vince lays out a playbook that drives consistency and equips reps to multi-thread and close complex enterprise deals."

— Kiva Kolstein,
CRO, Gold Stevie Winner

"Vince delivers more than inspiration, he provides a structured, zone-based framework that sales teams can apply immediately and consistently."

— Steve Richard,
Co-Founder Vorsight, Sales Expert

"Every top seller needs a playbook but even more, they need the instincts to call the right play. Red Zone Selling shows you how to think, execute, and win like a pro."

— Richard Harris,
5x AAiSP Top Sales Leader

"Great sales is all about calling the right play at the right time, and Vince Beese knows how to call the plays."

— Neil Weitzman,
Fractional CRO at Weitzman GTM

"Vince delivers a winner's blueprint - elite closers recognize momentum, control the moment, and execute when it matters most."

— Gal Aga,
CEO at Aligned

"This book is clear, real, and immediately useful. Vince doesn't waste your time with jargon or fluff. He hands you a playbook you'll actually use whether you're closing deals yourself or coaching others to do it."

— Randi-Sue Deckard,
SVP Growth at Beseler,
and Founder at Wednesday Women

"Red Zone Selling outlines how strategic sellers can eliminate the pressure and complexity that come with the territory by staying in control of the game and running actionable plays and drills for each stage or "zone" of the buying journey. As an enterprise seller, this is the book I wish I'd had years ago. I'm excited to implement it in my current process, and if you want to sell more, you should too."

— Jesse Woodbury,
Enterprise Account Executive,
Startup Sales Expert & Founder of Sales Players

"Sales is a game of execution. With Red Zone Selling, Vince Beese has written a fantastic playbook to help sellers think like top athletes - utilizing the right plays at the right time with certainty and using mindset strategies for success. Perfect your activities in the Yellow Zone, and then Green, to win in the Red Zone."

— Lori Richardson,
Score More Sales, 4x Salesforce Top Influencer

"Sales success isn't magic - it comes from consistently executing on the fundamentals from your first engagement with a prospect to the very last closing conversation. Vince has created a fantastic step-by-step playbook that clearly outlines what you need to do to "move the ball". Read this, learn the plays, and guide your customers over the goal line more quickly and more often."

— David J.P. Fisher,
author of *Hyper-Connected Selling*

RED ZONE SELLING

RED ZONE SELLING

The Ultimate Playbook for
High-Performing Enterprise Sellers

VINCE BEESE

JONES MEDIA
PUBLISHING

Jones Media Publishing
10645 N. Tatum Blvd. Ste. 200-166
Phoenix, AZ 85028
JonesMediaPublishing.com

Disclaimer:

The author strives to be as accurate and complete as possible in the creation of this book, notwithstanding the fact that the author does not warrant or represent at any time that the contents within are accurate due to the rapidly changing nature of the Internet. While all attempts have been made to verify information provided in this publication, the Author and the Publisher assume no responsibility and are not liable for errors, omissions, or contrary interpretation of the subject matter herein. The Author and Publisher hereby disclaim any liability, loss or damage incurred as a result of the application and utilization, whether directly or indirectly, of any information, suggestion, advice, or procedure in this book. Any perceived slights of specific persons, peoples, or organizations are unintentional.

In practical advice books, like anything else in life, there are no guarantees of income made. Readers are cautioned to rely on their own judgment about their individual circumstances to act accordingly. Readers are responsible for their own actions, choices, and results. This book is not intended for use as a source of legal, business, accounting or financial advice. All readers are advised to seek the services of competent professionals in legal, business, accounting, and finance field.

Printed in the United States of America

Want more tools to help you close like a
Red Zone sales pro?

Get free access to the Red Zone Selling Resource
Center, templates, scripts, and playbooks, when you
join the Red Zone Selling community.

Start now at redzoneselling.co.

Dedicated to the career sales professionals, the ones who show up every day ready to compete, who thrive under pressure, and who never stop chasing the win. Your grit, resilience, and drive to get better are what make this game great. Here's to those who live in the Red Zone.

Table of Contents

Acknowledgements

I want to sincerely thank my wife, Alene, for her unwavering support in all my endeavors, including the long hours and late nights spent bringing *Red Zone Selling* to life. I'm deeply grateful to Andy Paul for his guidance over the years, and to Justin Michael for giving me the courage to put this playbook into the world. And to the sales professionals who continue to inspire, teach, and motivate me each and every day.

Introduction

Red Zone Selling

Imagine your team is in the Super Bowl. It's the fourth quarter, and you're down by four. The clock is ticking. You've driven all the way down the field, and now you're in the Red Zone just ten yards from victory. Every decision matters. One mistake, and the opportunity is gone. But the great quarterbacks? They don't panic. They execute. They know exactly what play to run, how to read the defense, and how to finish strong.

Sales is no different. You've worked the deal for months, maybe a year. You've built relationships, qualified the opportunity, and presented a strong case for why your solution is the right fit. Then . . . the deal stalls. A prospect hesitates. A competitor sneaks in at the last minute.

Most sales professionals don't lose deals because of price, product, or competition. They lose because they fail to control the game from start to finish. They play defense instead of offense, reacting rather than dictating the pace.

This book will change that.

Elite quarterbacks dictate the tempo of the game, read the defense, and make the right call at the right time. Red Zone Selling is your playbook for doing the same in sales.

This isn't just another sales methodology, it's a game plan to help you:

- Take control of the sales process from first contact to final signature.
- Eliminate stalls by keeping momentum high and addressing objections early.
- Close deals faster and more consistently with a repeatable, high-impact framework.

In football, the Red Zone, is the final 20 yards before the end zone, is where the pressure is highest. Other sports have their version of a Red Zone as well, the last five minutes of a basketball or hockey game, serving out a match in tennis, closing out in the bottom of the 9th inning in baseball, or running the last mile of a marathon. Sales has its own version of the Red Zone: the final stretch of a deal where every move matters.

Sales are won or lost in the final stretch of the Red Zone where urgency is high, competition is fierce, and execution makes the difference between winning and losing. The strategies in this book will teach you how to navigate every stage of the deal like an elite closer, ensuring you never let a winnable opportunity slip away.

The truth is, you don't win in the Red Zone unless you've played the right way to get to the Red Zone. That's why Red Zone Selling is a framework for the entire sales process, not just the close. It breaks the sales cycle into three key zones, each mapped to a stage of the buyer's journey:

- **Yellow Zone** (Qualification Zone) – Validate the opportunity, identify decision-makers, and disqualify bad leads early.
- **Green Zone** (Momentum Zone) – Build alignment, guide the buying process, and prevent deals from stalling.
- **Red Zone** (Closing Zone) – Execute the final steps, overcome last-minute objections, and close with precision.

If you can master these three zones, you'll take control of your deals, eliminate uncertainty, and close with confidence.

Each chapter in this book will provide real-world strategies, actionable plays, and proven techniques that you can implement immediately. You'll learn:

- How to dictate the pace of a deal, instead of reacting to the buyer's timeline.
- How to remove friction and keep deals moving forward.
- How to execute with confidence when it's time to close.

By the end of this book, you'll have a repeatable system for winning more deals, more often. You'll become an elite "play caller."

The best athletes execute under pressure and thrive in high-stakes moments. The best sales professionals do the same.

Sales Found Me

One last thing before we dive in. I didn't grow up dreaming of a sales career or aspiring to be a sales leader. No, my first dream was to be a starting linebacker for the New York Giants, someone like Lawrence Taylor or Harry Carson. But given my size, that was never in the cards. My next best option? Sports broadcasting. Strike two. With no real prospects in that field, I answered a different kind of calling, or more accurately, a call.

I responded to a job ad looking for "sports-minded" people. That had to be me, right? I mean, I was *almost* a linebacker for the Giants. I landed the job as a fresh-faced Account Executive, a title I had never even heard of at the time. My task? Sell advertising for a brand-new magazine called *Washington Entertainment* in D.C. There was no formal sales training, just a phone book and a directive to start dialing. Figuring out how to sell was entirely on me.

We had a small team, and like most sales organizations, we tracked our stats on a leaderboard. I wasn't the guy with the most opportunities, the most appointments, or even the most callbacks. But I did lead in one category: *closed deals*.

Fast forward twenty-five plus years. I've helped scale five companies to successful exits, generated over a billion dollars in revenue, closed deals with hundreds of companies, and mentored countless sales professionals and leaders. These experiences shaped the foundation of Red Zone Selling, a proven framework for closing deals with precision and consistency.

Whether you're just starting out in sales, an experienced enterprise seller, a founder leading sales or a seasoned sales leader, Red Zone Selling is your playbook to becoming an elite closer. Ready? Let's get to work.

Next, I'll introduce you to the Red Zone Playbook, and you'll learn how to systematically advance every deal to the finish line.

CHAPTER 1

The Red Zone Playbook

Your Framework to Winning More Deals

Every team sport has a playbook. Whether it's football, baseball, basketball, soccer, volleyball, or hockey, teams rely on structured game plans to maximize their chances of winning. A playbook ensures that every player knows their role, executes with precision, and adapts to different situations. It also helps coaches teach fundamentals and refine techniques to increase performance. Without a playbook, teams rely on guesswork instead of strategy, leading to inconsistency and missed opportunities. Sales is no different.

Throughout my career in enterprise sales, at companies like LivePerson, CheetahMail, SugarCRM, True Fit, Kustomer, and Meta, 1 saw that having a structured approach was essential. Closing seven-figure deals and generating over a billion in revenue wasn't luck; it was the result of a proven system. A playbook kept me focused, helped me navigate complex deals, and ensured I was always prepared with the right move at the right time. This experience inspired me to create Red Zone Selling.

Did you know that an NFL playbook contains between 300 and 1,000 plays, depending on the team's offensive and defensive complexity? Each week, coaches tailor their game plan to include around 75 to 100 plays designed specifically for that week's opponent. Imagine having to memorize 75 plays every single game! That's why quarterbacks wear wristbands with the play calls. They need quick access to the right play in high-pressure moments.

On game day, an NFL team runs between 60 and 70 offensive plays, adjusting based on tempo, game flow, and time of possession. High-tempo offenses might push past 75 plays, while slower, run-heavy teams may run closer to 55. Across both teams, an NFL game typically includes 120 to 140 offensive plays.

Now, think about enterprise sales. If an NFL quarterback needs a structured playbook to execute in real-time, why would a salesperson navigate high-stakes deals without one?

The Closer's Playbook

Red Zone Selling is your playbook. It provides the framework for running the right play, at the right time, in the right situation, helping you close deals with confidence and consistency. But this isn't a one-size-fits-all model. Just like NFL teams customize their playbooks, you'll need to adapt Red Zone Selling to fit your sales process, industry, and customers.

Sales is a game of execution. The best reps don't wing it. They don't rely on charisma, luck, or a clever subject line. They operate with precision, clarity, and control, especially when it matters most. Yet, too many deals fall apart because there's no real system guiding the rep. One week there's momentum; the next it's silence. One meeting has the buying team leaning in; the next it's: *we need more time.* The problem isn't usually the product, pricing, or even competition. It's the lack of a consistent, structured approach to move a deal forward from first contact to final signature.

That's where Red Zone Selling comes in.

Red Zone Selling isn't another abstract methodology. It's a practical game plan for closing more deals by aligning your sales approach with the actual journey your prospects go through. It breaks the process down into manageable zones so you know exactly what to do at each stage, and just as important, what not to do.

The inspiration for this framework comes from what happens in the most high-pressure moments of any competitive game: the Red Zone.

Picture this. It's the final drive of a playoff game. The score is tied. The offense is inside the 20-yard line, deep in the Red Zone. There's under a minute left on the clock, no timeouts, and everything is on the line. The defense tightens. The crowd is deafening. The coaches are holding their breath.

This is where elite quarterbacks rise.

Former New England Patriots superstar Tom Brady built a career on moments like this, methodically advancing the ball, reading the defense, adjusting at the line of scrimmage, and delivering under pressure. The San Francisco 49ers' Joe Montana once led a 92-yard game-winning drive in the Super Bowl with ice in his veins, famously spotting John Candy in the stands to calm his teammates before dropping a perfect pass into the end zone. The Kansas City Chiefs Patrick Mahomes routinely turns broken plays into magic in the final seconds, extending drives with his feet, reading coverages mid-play, and making throws that most quarterbacks wouldn't even attempt.

These moments are not won by accident. They're won through preparation, situational awareness, and execution when it matters most. The greats know the playbook cold, but more importantly, they know when to stick with it, when to call an audible, and when to improvise.

Sales is no different. You can do everything right for 80 percent of the deal, and still lose in the final 20 yards. Red Zone Selling gives you the structure and mindset to finish strong. It helps you recognize where your deal is, what play to run, and how to keep control.

Red Zone Selling breaks the sales process into three distinct zones. Each one corresponds to a stage in the customer journey, and each one requires a different set of plays, strategies, and mindsets.

RED ZONE PLAYBOOK

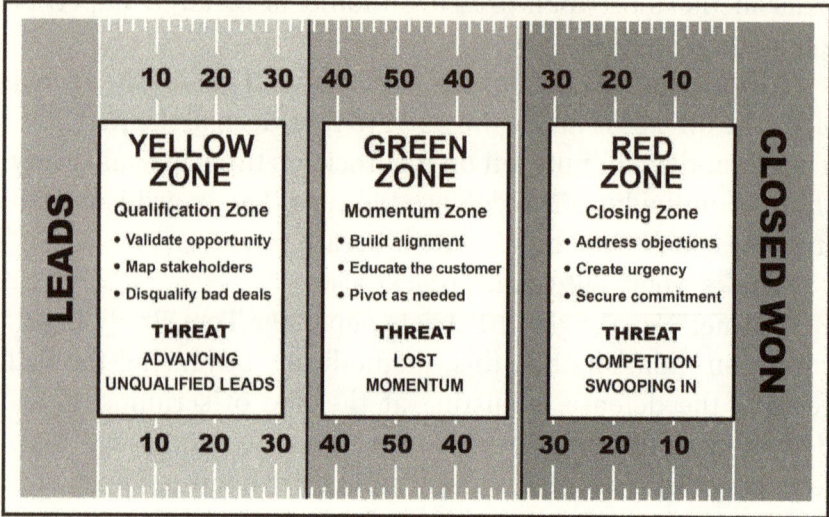

| LEADS | YELLOW ZONE | GREEN ZONE | RED ZONE | CLOSED WON |

Visualizes the Red Zone Selling framework mapped to a football field, emphasizing strategic movement through Yellow, Green, and Red Zones.

The Yellow Zone is the Qualification Zone

This is where you validate the opportunity. Are you chasing a deal that's worth your time? Is this the right customer profile? Do they have a real problem and budget to solve it? Can you access the decision-makers? This is where you get your read on the field. Fail here, and you're setting yourself up for wasted effort.

The Green Zone is the Momentum Zone

The prospect is interested. You've made it past the first few downs. You're in the middle of the field. But this is where most deals stall. You start hearing: *Let me circle back.* Or: *We need more time.* The buyer seems engaged, but you're not moving forward. The key in the Green Zone is to keep momentum alive. You need to keep building urgency, aligning stakeholders, and removing friction. This is where the deal gains, or loses, speed.

The Red Zone is the Closing Zone

You've made it to the final stretch. The proposal is out, the stakeholder alignment is strong, and you're preparing for signatures. This is where the pressure peaks. Legal gets involved. Procurement raises flags. A competitor tries to sneak in at the last second. The buyer suddenly goes quiet.

Welcome to the Red Zone. This is where execution separates closers from everyone else. You need focus, urgency, and precision. You're either walking away with a signed contract, or you face the painful refrain: *We decided to go in a different direction.*

The best sellers know which zone they're in *at all times.* They don't run the same play in the Yellow Zone as they do in the Red Zone. They adapt. They read the field. They call the right play, not just the familiar one.

That's what Red Zone Selling teaches you to do.

In the next three chapters, we'll take a deep dive into each zone. Chapter Two will focus entirely on the Yellow Zone. You'll learn how to qualify like a pro, ask the right questions, identify real pain, and disqualify deals early that are going nowhere. You'll get specific plays for validating ideal customer profiles, stakeholder mapping, and effective disqualification. These are the skills that save time and create focus.

In Chapter Three, we'll go into the Green Zone. This is where most deals slow down or fall apart. You'll learn how to keep deals moving, how to multi-thread effectively, and how to run plays that prevent deals from stalling. We'll talk about how to build alignment across multiple stakeholders, how to anticipate objections, and how to test deal commitment early.

Chapter Four will cover the Red Zone, the last push. This is where you apply pressure without being pushy. It's where you handle last-minute objections with confidence. It's where you don't just ask for the sale, you assume it. You'll learn how to run final-close plays that work under pressure. You'll know how to identify and remove last-second blockers. And, you'll be prepared to finish strong without discounting your value.

Each chapter includes subtopics that break the zone into smaller, manageable areas of focus. Each subtopic is accompanied by tactical plays you can run, repeatable actions and strategies that have worked in high-pressure, real-world enterprise sales environments. These are not theoretical ideas. These are the same plays I used to close complex, multi-stakeholder, seven-figure deals.

Each individual chapter also include specific drills to help you put these concepts into practice. These are exercises you can use solo or with your team to refine your skills, test your approach, and sharpen execution.

Mindset Matters

This chapter is the exception. This chapter is about mindset. This chapter is your blueprint.

Think of this as your pregame speech and your field map. It's meant to orient you, so that when we get into the tactical zone work, you'll know exactly why it matters.

Because here's the reality: Most salespeople don't lose deals because they lack skill or effort. They lose deals because they don't know what's really happening in the deal cycle. They're running plays from the wrong zone. They're guessing. And when it gets tough, they default to discounts, pressure tactics, or waiting.

Red Zone Selling helps you stop guessing.
You'll learn how to:

- Qualify with precision instead of wasting time.
- Maintain control throughout the buyer journey.
- Navigate the inevitable slowdowns and stalls.
- Close with urgency, confidence, and intention.

You're not just a salesperson, you're the quarterback. You set the pace. You read the defense. You call the play.

This book is your wristband. It's your playbook. It's your sideline coach.

And the next three chapters are where the game really begins.

Ready? Let's take the field.

Get access to the Red Zone Selling Resource Center including templates, scripts, and playbooks at redzoneselling.co.

CHAPTER 2

Yellow Zone

The Qualification Zone

During the 1989 Super Bowl, legend has it that as Joe Montana, quarterback of the San Francisco 49ers, stepped onto the field for the game's final drive, looked into the huddle, smiled, and casually pointed toward the crowd.

"Hey, is that John Candy?" he asked his teammates.

Think about that for a second. Montana's team was trailing 16–13. They were backed up on their own 8-yard line. The Super Bowl was on the line. The world was watching. And here's Joe Cool, cracking a joke about spotting a movie star in the crowd.

But that wasn't a distraction. It was control. Total command of the moment.

Montana wasn't rattled. He wasn't overwhelmed. He wasn't guessing. He had already read the field, understood the defense, and locked into the opportunity in front of him. That calm confidence, the clarity under pressure, is what made him great. And it's the exact mindset you need in the Yellow Zone.

What followed that moment became legend. Eleven plays. Ninety-two yards. With 39 seconds left, Montana fired a strike to John Taylor in the end zone, giving the 49ers a 20–16 lead and securing another Super Bowl title.

Now here's what most people miss about that story. It wasn't just the final throw that made Montana great: *It was how he started the drive.* Montana didn't come to the line panicking. He didn't run a desperation play. He read the defense. He looked for the safeties. He identified matchups. He scanned for coverage patterns. Then he executed, one play at a time. He didn't force the win. He worked the drive with discipline and intention.

That's exactly what elite sales professionals do in the Yellow Zone.

The Yellow Zone is your pre-snap read. It's the moment in a deal where you decide if this is a real opportunity or just a distraction.

Most reps want to move fast. They want to jump right to the pitch, to the demo, to the proposal. But that's like throwing a Hail Mary on the first play.

The Yellow Zone exists to slow you down, just enough to think clearly.

This is where you qualify with precision. You don't just take interest at face value. You ask yourself:

- *Does this prospect fit our Ideal Customer Profile (ICP)?*
- *Is there real pain, or are they just browsing?*
- *Are we speaking with someone who actually has influence?*
- *What does the internal decision-making process look like?*
- *Should I advance this opportunity or kill it now?*

If you can't answer those questions early, you're driving blind.

Montana didn't throw the game-winning pass on play one. He moved the chains. He picked up chunks of yardage. He stayed ahead of the defense.

That's what qualifying is.

THE ZONES

GOAL LINE	LEAD	PROB%
10	YELLOW ZONE	10%
20	Qualification	20%
30		30%
	GREEN ZONE	
40		40%
50	Momentum	50%
40		60%
30		70%
20	RED ZONE	80%
10	Closing	90%
END ZONE	CLOSED WON	100%

Like driving down the field, each zone demands a strategy and plays to keep momentum and close the deal.

Every discovery call, every early email, every stakeholder you engage is a read, a way to assess the field before you commit to the full drive.

The biggest mistake average salespeople make is confusing interest for intent.

Someone agreeing to a meeting isn't a sign to celebrate. It's a signal to investigate.

That's what the Yellow Zone is all about. Before you invest hours building a proposal, pulling in engineering, scheduling executives, you need to know if the field is clear.

Are you running a clean drive? Or, are you heading into a stacked defense, with no chance to score?

The best salespeople don't chase everything. They qualify ruthlessly. They walk away from bad fits.

They know that false opportunities are the biggest threat to real ones. Just like Montana wouldn't throw into triple coverage just to prove a point, elite sellers don't pursue a deal just because someone's willing to talk.

They play to win, not just to move the ball.

In the Yellow Zone, you're not closing, you're reading. You're listening. You're eliminating noise and locking in on the right opportunity. Because the truth is, you don't win deals in the Red Zone unless you qualify them correctly in the Yellow Zone.

So let's break down how to run your opening plays like a Hall of Fame quarterback, clear-eyed, disciplined, and focused on the win.

Let's break down the three biggest plays in the Yellow Zone.

Run the Right Route: Stick to Your ICP

In football, not every play works against every defense. You design plays that match the coverage. The same goes for sales. You don't sell to everyone, you sell to the right ones.

That's where your Ideal Customer Profile (ICP) comes in. It's your offensive scheme. Your playbook filter. Your ICP is a clear definition of the companies where you win most often, based on data, not hope. It includes such factors as industry, company size, revenue range, geography, tech stack, buying triggers, and typical use cases. If a prospect doesn't fit your ICP, they're not worth the reps, resources, or risk.

Why It Matters: Wasting time on bad-fit leads kills close rates. Your pipeline fills with fluff, your forecasts get bloated, and your win rate tanks. Selling to someone just because they'll take a meeting isn't a qualification, it's a gamble.

Play 1: The ICP Alignment Play

What: Assess whether the company fits your Ideal Customer Profile by checking:

- **Industry:** Do they operate in a space you win in consistently?

- **Company Size:** Are they within your sweet spot (revenue, headcount, growth stage)?

- **Tech Stack:** Is your solution compatible with their environment?

- **Use Case:** Do they have a clear, winnable problem you solve better than anyone?

- **Urgency Profile:** Are there signs of internal pressure, timelines, or pain to act?

If the answer is "no" to most of these, qualify out early.

Why: Top sellers don't waste time on accounts they're not built to win. Chasing poor-fit deals leads to longer sales cycles, lower win rates, and constant frustration. Your ICP isn't just a marketing tool, it's your targeting system. If you go off course, you're playing someone else's game.

Example: Your team thrives in mid-market B2B Software as a Service (SaaS). A massive logistics enterprise reaches out. It looks exciting, but they're outside your lane: different industry, complex systems, long procurement cycles. It might sound like an opportunity, but in reality, it's a distraction that eats pipeline health and wastes your best closing windows.

Pro Tip: One of the fastest ways to increase your win rate is by disqualifying early and often. Focus deals with a good ICP fit, and your pipeline will get smaller, but more winnable. That's how pros close more with less.

ICP ALIGNMENT SCORECARD

CATEGORY	QUALIFYING QUESTION	WINNING CRITERIA	YOUR NOTES / SCORE (1-5)
Industry	Do they operate in a space we consistently win in?	Industry matches our proven customer base.	
Company Size	Are they in our sweet spot (revenue, head-count, growth stage?	Aligned with our ICP range (e.g. 100-1000 employees, Series B+)	
Tech Stack	Is our solution compatible with their environment?	Compatible tech-minimal friction to implement	
Use Case	Do they have a problem we solve better than anyone else?	Clear, urgent use case aligned to our core value proposition	

Use the ICP Alignment Scorecard to quickly qualify opportunities and stay focused on high-probability wins.

Play 2: The Priority Fit Play

What: Ask early: *Where does this initiative rank on your priority list this quarter?*

Follow up by probing for budget timing, executive involvement, or internal urgency drivers. If your solution isn't tied to a strategic objective or active pain, deprioritize, or set a future trigger.

Why: Even if an account fits your Ideal Customer Profile, that doesn't mean they're ready to buy. If your solution isn't in their top three initiatives this quarter, it won't get resources, attention, or velocity. You're qualifying for urgency, not just fit. Sellers lose valuable time by chasing the right company with the wrong timing.

Example: You're talking to a prospect in your ICP who's curious about automation. Everything sounds good, until they reveal that their top priorities this quarter are reducing churn and expanding into a new market. Process automation? It's a "nice to have" for next year. You've just uncovered why this deal will stall before it starts.

Pro Tip: The Yellow Zone is where you diagnose, not pitch. Think like a doctor. Ask before you prescribe. If you skip this and jump into a demo or solutioning too quickly, you'll be solving problems they aren't ready, or motivated, to fix.

Diagnose the Pain Before You Prescribe

Before you can prescribe a solution, you need to understand how badly the problem hurts. Most sellers stop at surface pain, but top performers dig deeper to uncover the true business impact. This play helps you go beyond curiosity and find out if there's real motivation to act.

The Yellow Zone is where you diagnose. You're not selling yet, you're listening, probing, understanding what really hurts.

Deals don't die because the product wasn't good. They die because the buyer didn't feel the pain deeply enough to act.

Surface-level interest won't carry a deal. You need to anchor it to real business consequences.

Play 3: The Deep Pain Probe

What: Use layered questions that push the buyer to reveal the business and personal cost of the problem, such as:

- *What happens if you don't fix this?*

- *Who feels this pain the most?*

- *Has this issue cost your team any revenue or time recently?*

- *What is the impact if you don't solve this problem?*

- *How have you tried to solve this in the past?*

Your goal is to anchor the pain to urgency and consequence.

Why: If there's no meaningful consequence to inaction, there's no urgency to buy. Buyers may show interest, but unless there's pain with weight behind it, lost revenue, time, or pressure from leadership, they won't move. This play gets to the emotional and financial root of the issue.

Example: Back when I was at Kustomer, we were working with a fast-growing e-commerce brand that was clearly outgrowing their current support platform. Their agents were juggling multiple tools and context switching constantly, but the leadership team wasn't feeling enough pain to make a change. During discovery, we asked: *What's the impact of sticking with your current setup for another quarter?* The answer was vague. So we stepped back, gave them space, and circled back three months later with a sharper pain probe. This time, we helped them quantify the missed SLAs, the rising churn, and the agent burnout. Suddenly, the cost of inaction was undeniable, and that deal closed fast.

Pro Tip: If the buyer says, *This would be nice to have,* stop the drive. That's not pain, it's preference. Great sellers know: No pain, no gain, no deal.

Once you've anchored the urgency with real, tangible pain, it's time to shift the focus, now we uncover what personal wins will truly motivate your buyer to act.

Play 4: The Personal Win Play

When buyers evaluate solutions, they're not just thinking about company performance, they're thinking about themselves. Titles might drive process, but personal wins drive urgency. This play helps you find what really motivates your champion beyond the business case.

What: Ask a simple but powerful question: *If this goes well, how does it impact you personally?*

Listen closely. You're looking for themes like visibility, credibility, reduced stress, or career growth. These personal wins become your leverage when the deal hits resistance or slows down.

Why: People make emotional decisions first and justify them with logic later. If your solution can help a buyer hit a personal goal, get promoted, prove a point, impress a boss, they're far more likely to push the deal forward, fight for budget, and bring others into the conversation.

Example: You're meeting with a RevOps director who says the current tools are inefficient. That's the business issue. But when you ask what success would look like for them personally, they say: *Honestly, if I roll this out cleanly, the CRO will finally trust me with next year's roadmap.* Now you're not just selling efficiency, you're helping them earn internal influence. That changes everything.

Pro Tip: People don't push deals across the finish line for features, they push for themselves. When the pressure is on, personal motivation is what keeps a deal alive. Don't sell to the role, sell to the human behind it.

Now that you've uncovered what drives your buyer personally, it's time to map the full field, because winning the deal means winning over the team behind the decision.

Play 5: The Triangle Map Play

Most deals fall apart not because the product fit isn't right, but because of a lack of people fit. You might be selling the perfect solution, but if you're not talking to the right roles, you're playing blind. This play gives you a fast and simple map to ensure you're building the relationships that actually move deals.

What: Identify and engage these three personas:

- **Economic Buyer:** Owns the budget and signs the check.

- **Technical Buyer:** Assesses solution feasibility, integration, and risk.

- **Champion:** Believes in your solution and will sell it internally on your behalf.

Ask your main contact: *Who's involved from a budget, technical, and day-to-day impact perspective?* This often opens up the internal map and reveals who you haven't met yet.

Why: Every healthy deal has three critical voices: the economic buyer, the technical buyer, and the champion. Each plays a different role in the decision process, budget, validation, and internal momentum. If one is missing or unknown, the deal is vulnerable. Mapping these roles early gives you clarity and control.

Example: You're in conversations with a marketing director who loves your product and wants to move forward. But when you ask about technical validation, they say: *Oh, IT will need to sign off at some point.*

That's your signal. The technical buyer is a silent veto if you don't loop them in early. One quick question just saved your deal from dying in Procurement.

Pro Tip: Invite the technical buyer to your discovery call whenever possible. It shows respect, speeds up evaluation, and reduces last-minute objections that could derail your close.

Once you've mapped the visible players, it's time to uncover the hidden influencers, the ones pulling strings behind the scenes.

HIGH AUTHORITY & INFLUENCE

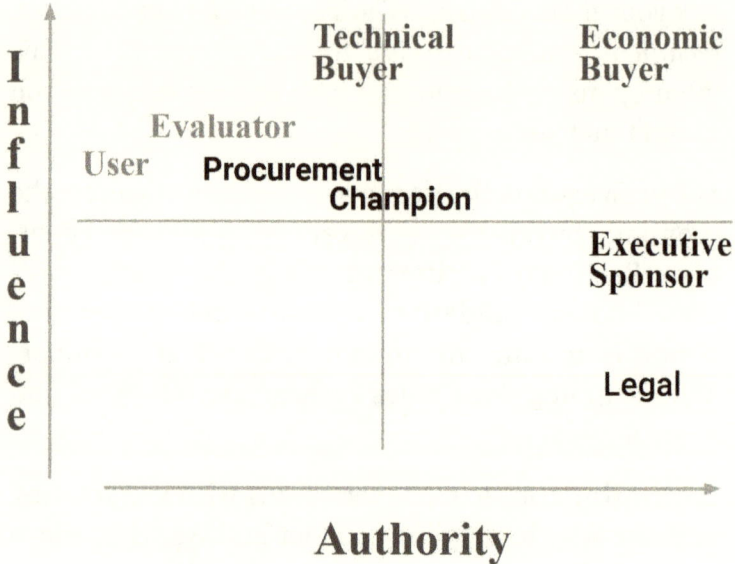

I n f l u e n c e

Technical Buyer

Economic Buyer

Evaluator

User   **Procurement**

Champion

Executive Sponsor

Legal

Authority

Stay Multi-thread by focusing on stakeholders with the most authority and influence.

Play 6: The Shadow Org Chart Play

In complex B2B sales, the org chart on LinkedIn is just the tip of the iceberg. Real influence often sits with unseen stakeholders, Compliance, Legal, IT, or political rivals. This play helps you surface the hidden players who can quietly kill your deal if you're not careful.

What: Ask your champion or main contact: *Who else has killed a deal like this in the past?* Follow up with: *Who would be upset if they weren't consulted?* You're not just building an org chart, you're uncovering the real map of influence, risk, and politics.

Why: Deals don't fall apart because of what you see, they fall apart because of what you *don't see*. It's that unexpected "SVP," Procurement hold-up, or quiet influencer who shows up late and slows or blocks the deal. Mapping power early protects your pipeline and prepares you for a smoother Red Zone close.

Example: You're deep into a deal with sales leadership and your champion is fully on board. Then Procurement pops up late with concerns about vendor history and forces a month-long legal delay. If you'd uncovered them in the Yellow Zone, you could have preemptively built buy-in. Instead, the deal slips to next quarter.

Pro Tip: Ask your champion to sketch the approval process, on paper, whiteboard, or email. Visual is always better than verbal. If they struggle to draw it, they don't really know the process, and that's your signal to dig deeper.

If you're constantly "working a deal" that goes nowhere, it's a Yellow Zone problem.

After identifying all the players, it's time to step back and assess: Is this deal even worth the pursuit? Let the 4F filter show you fast.

Play 7: The Simple Fit Formula: 4F Deal Filter

Qualification isn't just about to whom you sell, it's about when and how. Even good-fit prospects can stall or waste time if they don't meet the right criteria. This play gives you a fast, practical framework for deciding whether a deal is truly worth your time.

What: Use this 4-point check to evaluate whether an opportunity is worth advancing.

- **Fit**, Do they match your Ideal Customer Profile (ICP) and Use Case?

- **Friction**, Are they easy to engage, or do they require dragging through every step?

- **Funding**, Do they have a clear budget or business case that justifies investment?

- **Forecast**, Is there urgency anchored to a date, i.e., implementation?

4F DEAL FILTER

FIT	FRICTION
ICP & Use Case	Engaged or Dragging
FUNDING	**FORECAST**
Budget Justification	Date Anchored Urgency

Use the 4F Deal Filter; Fit, Friction, Funding, Forecast, to qualify fast and focus on the right opportunities.

If the deal scores at least three out of four, you've got something worth pursuing.

If it only hits one or two, it's time to either reposition, or walk away.

Why: Too many reps confuse activity with progress. They chase deals with low probability and then wonder why the quarter slipped. The 4F Filter helps you spot high-quality deals early, so you can focus on what closes and move on from what doesn't.

Example: You're speaking with a marketing VP who loves your solution. Fit and use case are strong, but when you ask about budget, they say, *It's not locked in,* and there's no implementation timeline. That's a 2 out of 4. Unless you can uncover urgency or activate funding, deprioritize and reallocate your energy elsewhere.

Pro Tip: Keep a running list of 4F-qualified deals. If a deal is not at least a 3, don't add it to your forecast. This play isn't about being negative, it's about being focused. Pipeline discipline is how closers stay in control.

Once you've qualified the deal with confidence, it's time to challenge it, because the best closers don't assume readiness, they pressure-test it.

Play 8: The Pressure-Test Close

Good sellers listen for interest. Great sellers test for intent. This play gives you a simple way to separate polite conversations from real buying energy, before you waste time running a full cycle for a deal that was never real.

What: Ask a direct alignment question: *If we can solve this problem, are you prepared to move forward this quarter?*

Variations can include:

- *Is this a must-solve now, or a nice-to-solve someday?*

- *What happens if this isn't implemented by [date]?*

You're testing for intent, not pushing for the close.

Why: Soft interest sounds like progress, but it's often a stall in disguise. If your buyer can't commit to next steps or urgency, you're not in a real deal. Pressure-testing early helps you qualify faster and avoid wasting your Red Zone energy on something that should've been disqualified in the Yellow Zone.

Example: You're working with a head of operations who's engaged, but vague on next steps. You ask: *If we solve this by the end of the quarter, are you ready to move forward?* They pause and say: *Honestly, this might get pushed to Q3.* That one question just saved you six weeks of chasing a ghost.

Pro Tip: Don't fear the answer. Clarity is always a win, whether it moves the deal forward or gives you permission to walk away. Confidence in the close starts with confidence in qualification.

If the deal holds up under pressure, the next move isn't to close, it's to qualify with conviction and align on the path forward. This play helps you drive that decision with clarity and control or walk away.

Play 9: The Kill-with-Confidence Script

Every minute you spend chasing an unwinnable deal is a minute you're not closing a real one. This play gives you a clean, professional way to walk away from bad-fit opportunities, without burning bridges or looking weak.

What: Use this language to confidently disqualify: *It sounds like this may not be the right time or fit. If that's the case, we'd rather step back than keep pushing something that won't deliver results.*

Be clear, respectful, and firm. You're not abandoning the deal, you're showing leadership by protecting both sides from wasted energy.

Why: Disqualifying isn't giving up, it's leveling up. Top performers know that strong qualification includes a strong exit strategy. When you take control and walk away from a bad deal, you earn respect, protect your pipeline, and often open the door for future re-engagement.

Example: You've had three meetings with a prospect who keeps pushing the timeline and isn't clear on internal priorities. You sense the interest is soft and there's no urgency. You deliver the line above. Now, instead of disappearing, they come back with: *Actually, we might be ready next quarter. Can we reconnect then?* You didn't lose the deal, you just stopped wasting time.

Pro Tip: Don't fear disqualification. Strong disqualification improves your close rate by focusing your time on deals that will actually close. It also positions you as a pro, someone who doesn't need the deal, but knows how to win the right ones.

With all nine plays on the field, you now have a complete system to assess fit, build alignment, and drive decisive next steps. Let's recap the key moves that set the foundation for momentum.

Chapter Recap

- The Yellow Zone is your pre-snap read: slow down, assess, and qualify with precision.
- Use your ICP like a playbook, If a prospect doesn't fit, don't force it.

- No pain means no movement. Dig until you find business consequences and personal wins.
- Stakeholder mapping wins deals. Talk to all decision-makers early, or risk getting blindsided.
- Use the 4F Deal Filter (Fit, Friction, Funding, Forecast) to assess whether to advance or disqualify.
- Don't fear walking away, It's much worse to waste time on a deal that's going nowhere.
- The faster you kill bad deals, the more time you have to win great ones.

Red Zone Drills:

Drill 1: 4F Filter Qualification

Pick five deals from your current pipeline. Do they hit three or four of the 4F Filter Questions? If so, then keep moving forward.

Drill 2: Deep Pain Questions

On your next discovery call, use this three-part sequence:

- *What's the core problem you're solving?*
- *What happens if you don't fix it?*
- *How does this affect you personally?*

Drill 3: Stakeholder Mapping Sprint

For every open deal, identify:

- The champion
- The economic buyer
- The technical evaluator

If any of these are missing, that's your next move.

Qualifying the right opportunities is just the beginning. Once you're lined up against the right opponent and you've read the field, it's time to move the ball down field, deliberately, strategically, and without losing momentum.

In the next chapter, we enter the Green Zone, where deals either gain traction or stall out. This is where execution separates top performers from the pack. Let's talk about how to build unstoppable momentum.

Get access to the Red Zone Selling Resource Center including templates, scripts, and playbooks at redzoneselling.co.

CHAPTER 3

Green Zone

The Momentum Zone

Improvising in sales is both under-taught and underutilized. The ability to think on your feet, adapt mid-play, and keep the deal moving forward when everything goes sideways, that's what separates elite sellers from the rest of the pack.

In football, nobody improvises better than Patrick Mahomes.

Watch him for a single drive and you'll see this in action. The play breaks down. The pocket collapses. A linebacker comes flying off the edge. Then just when you think the play is over, boom. Mahomes spins out, flips the ball underhand, or side-arms a dart to the back of the end zone. He doesn't panic. He keeps his head up. He reads the field. He finds a way to make something happen.

That's exactly what great salespeople do in the Green Zone.

You can have the perfect game plan, scripted discovery, polished decks, pain-aligned messaging, but, in real life, deals don't always follow the script. Sometimes champions leave. Budgets shift. Priorities get reshuffled. The buyers you've worked months to align suddenly ghost you, or worse, change direction. In those moments, you have two choices: freeze and hope it works out. . . or improvise and take control.

I learned this firsthand on a major enterprise deal with a global sportswear brand. It was a marquee account. High visibility. Career-defining stuff.

We were deep in the deal. The discovery had been tight, the demo was lights out, and we had strong buy-in from key stakeholders. Our champion, a rising leader in digital innovation, was helping push the deal through Procurement and navigating internal conversations with the Legal department. Everything felt aligned. The momentum was real. We were in the Green Zone, maybe even approaching the Red.

And then, just like that, he was gone.

New role. Different company. No warning. No handoff.

We were dead in the water.

The new leadership team had different priorities. They hadn't been part of the conversations. They didn't see the value. And, just like that, months of progress started slipping away. Our internal momentum evaporated.

That was the moment where we had to make a quick decision. Do we try to force the old narrative and hope it lands? Or do we pivot, fast?

We chose to adapt.

We paused the deal. This allowed us to rebuild the business case from scratch, this time anchored to the new leadership's vision. We stopped talking about what our former champion wanted and instead focused on what the new guard needed. We re-engaged procurement, looped in cross-functional stakeholders, and rebuilt momentum thread-by-thread. It was slow. It was gritty. But it worked. That deal eventually closed, and it turned out to be larger than we'd originally scoped.

It was not because we had the perfect plan. But because we didn't cling to that plan when the play collapsed.

That's what the Green Zone demands.

Momentum isn't a straight line and selling is not linear. It's messy. Dynamic. Often unpredictable. But what matters isn't perfection, it's progression. Your ability to keep the drive alive when the defense throws something new at you.

This chapter is about learning to improvise like Mahomes. It's about staying in motion when others would stall. It's about reading the field, adjusting the play, and advancing the deal, one first down at a time.

Because, in the Green Zone, deals don't die from a lack of effort. They die when momentum is lost . . . and no one knows how to get it back.

Let's break down how to keep moving, adapt under pressure, and control the mid-field like a pro.

The Momentum Zone: Advance or Die — The Power of Micro-Commitments

The Green Zone is where most deals stall, not because the buyer says *no*, but because the rep doesn't get a real *yes*.

Momentum can die slowly. It fades. Conversations fizzle. Prospects disappear.

Why? Because too many sellers leave meetings without a clear next step. They think the deal is moving when, in reality, it's stuck.

That's why micro-commitments matter. They're the short-yardage gains that keep the chains moving. In football terms, they're your 3rd-and-short conversion. They don't win the game, but they keep the drive alive.

Why It Matters: Deals that stall in the Green Zone often don't come back. When there's no next action, time kills urgency. Competitors sneak in. Priorities shift. And suddenly, a hot deal turns cold.

Momentum isn't built through energy, it's built through movement. That means every meeting, email, and conversation must drive to the next step.

That's what the Green Zone is all about, creating consistent forward motion. Let's kick it off with the first play to keep deals from stalling.

Play 1: The Scheduled Next Step Play

What: Never end a meeting without putting the next one on the calendar. Confirm the time, agenda, and who will attend.

Why: A deal without a scheduled next step is not a deal, it's a loose thread. Locking in the next step keeps accountability and visibility in place.

Pro Tip: Even if the meeting is two weeks out, schedule it anyway. You can always move it. But unscheduled means uncertain.

Once there's alignment on the problem and direction, the next move is locking in the path forward, together. That's where the Mutual Action Plan comes in.

Play 2: The Mutual Action Plan Play

What: Co-create a timeline with your buyer that outlines key milestones, technical review, stakeholder approvals, legal review, procurement steps, and final signature.

Why: When buyers help build the plan, they become more invested in its success. Shared ownership creates natural urgency, keeps everyone aligned, and reduces the risk of delays and last-minute surprises.

How to Build It (Step-by-Step):

1. Start with the End in Mind: Ask the buyer, *"When do you want this solution live and delivering value?"* Work backward from that date.

2. Identify Key Milestones: Collaborate on critical steps, security reviews, legal redlines, budget approvals, training, etc.

3. Assign Ownership: For each step, confirm who's responsible on both sides. If names aren't available yet, list roles (e.g., "VP Finance").

4. Set Target Dates: These are commitments, not guesses. Dates create momentum. Use language like, *"Can we aim for this to be wrapped up by [date]?"*

5. Use a Shared Workspace: Build it in a mutual tool (e.g., Google Doc, Notion, or your CRM). Ensure it's accessible and editable by both parties.

6. Make It a Living Document: Revisit the plan weekly. Use it to steer meetings, manage accountability, and address slippage early.

Example:

During a complex enterprise sale, a rep worked with their champion to map out every approval needed. They set target dates for each step and updated the plan weekly. As a result, the deal closed two weeks earlier than forecasted because the buyer was motivated to stay on track.

Pro Tip: Use shared documents or tools like Google Docs, Notion, or your CRM to build the action plan. Make it a living document that both sides can view and update in real time, increasing collaboration and visibility.

With a Mutual Action Plan in place, it's important to keep the momentum alive and ensure everyone stays aligned. The next step is using a Progress Recap Email to reinforce the plan, highlight wins, and prevent deals from stalling.

Play 3: The Progress Recap Email

What: After every meeting, send a concise follow-up email summarizing what was discussed, any decisions made, and the next one or two action items.

Why: A clear recap keeps everyone aligned, shows professionalism, and creates a documented trail. It also helps prevent ghosting by signaling that you're driving the process forward with clarity and intent, like a pro quarterback reading the field, not a rookie hoping for a play.

Example: After a discovery call with a buying committee, the rep sent a recap within an hour: *Here's what we covered, here's what we agreed on, and here's what's next.* The deal stayed hot because the buyer didn't have to guess what was coming, they already had the playbook.

Pro Tip: Use tools like Fathom or Fireflies to record and summarize calls automatically. Pull the key points and proposed next steps into your email for fast, accurate follow-up that builds trust and keeps momentum.

Now that you've got the plan and communication rhythm in place, it's time to level up your deal control. The next move? Multi-threading like a pro, because relying on one contact is like running a one-receiver offense. Too risky. Let's spread the field.

Play 4: Multi-Thread Like a Pro:
Engage the Buying Committee

If you're relying on one contact to push your deal forward, you're one Slack message away from being irrelevant. Single-threaded deals die slow, quiet deaths, usually in a meeting to which you were not invited.

That's why multi-threading matters. In the Green Zone, your job is to get the entire offense on the field. You don't win by throwing to one receiver. You win by spreading the ball around.

Why It Matters: Most B2B deals involve six to ten stakeholders. If you're not talking to multiple decision-makers, you're not really in the deal, you're just hoping someone else sells it for you.

Multi-threading de-risks the opportunity, uncovers objections early, and increases internal momentum by getting more people aligned to your value. Think of multi-threading as an insurance policy in case your champion leaves or you have an insider that isn't a promoter.

> **What:** Go beyond your primary contact and build relationships with all key stakeholders involved in the deal. That includes the executive sponsor, champion, economic buyer, technical buyer, evaluators, procurement contacts, and any potential blockers.
>
> **Why:** Single-threaded deals are high risk. If your only contact goes quiet or loses influence, your deal stalls, or dies. Multi-threading expands your influence, uncovers competing priorities, and builds internal momentum. It ensures you're not just selling to one person, but selling *with* an internal team.

Example: An AE selling to a mid-market SaaS company was working solely with her champion in marketing. By asking, "Who else is involved in approving this?" she uncovered the economic buyer (CFO), the technical buyer (IT Director), and the executive sponsor (COO). She built a stakeholder map, tailored her messaging to each persona, and turned a mid-size deal into a company-wide rollout by aligning everyone around a shared business case.

How to Map Key Stakeholders:

Use a simple visual or spreadsheet to map the people involved in the deal. Start with these roles:

- **Executive Sponsor**: Has the authority and vision to greenlight the deal; usually at the VP or C-level.

- **Champion:** Your internal advocate who wants the solution and is pushing it forward.

- **Economic Buyer:** Controls the budget; needs to be convinced of ROI and strategic value.

- **Technical Buyer:** Evaluates whether your solution fits within their existing systems and infrastructure.

- **Evaluator(s):** Hands-on users or analysts comparing your solution to others.

- **Procurement Team:** Final gatekeeper on contracts, pricing, and terms.

- **Potential Blockers:** Anyone who could slow or kill the deal due to competing priorities, past experiences, or perceived risk.

MAPPING THE KEY STAKEHOLDERS INTERNALLY

Name	Title	Role	Strategic Position	Influence	Coverage
John Smith	VP of CX	Champion	Promoter	High	Mary
Jill Olsen	User	Influencer	Promoter	Medium	Jim
Bill Lynn	IT Dir	Technical Buyer	Threat	Medium	Sue
Sallie Mae	SVP	Economic Buyer	Neutral	High	Vince

*Map key stakeholders and assign internal owners
to drive alignment and accountability.*

Track their influence, role, attitude (supportive, neutral, resistant), and what matters most to them. This gives you a strategic view of how to navigate the internal politics of the deal.

Pro Tip: Don't ask: *Who's the decision-maker?* Instead, ask:

- *Who else needs to weigh in before this moves forward?*

- *Who else is impacted by this change?*

You'll get more honest answers and uncover the real buying dynamics.

Once you've mapped the key players, it's time to start building real connections. The fastest path to warm introductions? Leverage your champion. That's where the champion Co-Intro Play comes in.

Play 5: The Champion Co-Intro Play

What: Ask your champion to introduce you to other stakeholders in their organization (e.g., IT, finance, end users, or the executive sponsor).

Why: Warm introductions carry more weight and build instant credibility. Instead of going around your champion (which can feel political), this play honors their role while expanding your influence. It also helps you multi-thread without triggering resistance.

Example: After a strong discovery call, a rep asked their champion: *Would you be open to introducing me to your IT counterpart so we can align on integration early?* The champion agreed and sent an intro email using the rep's draft. That intro unlocked the technical buyer, who helped accelerate the security review and smoothed the path to close.

Pro Tip: Make it easy for your champion to help you. Send them a short email draft, message, or one-sentence value summary they can copy and paste. The less friction, the more likely they'll follow through, and quickly.

Also, align key stakeholders to executives at your company, i.e. your CTO to their IT head, your founder to their founder, etc.

Now that you've started connecting with more stakeholders, it's crucial to keep everyone on the same page. That's where the Alignment Summary Play comes in, your tool for reinforcing clarity, buy-in, and next steps across the board.

Play 6: The Alignment Summary Play

What: Build a clear alignment summary, one page or slide deck, that connects your solution to the specific priorities of each stakeholder in the deal. This includes a simple, credible business case showing how your offering drives measurable impact, especially in areas like cost savings, efficiency gains, or revenue growth.

Why: Champions don't close deals, committees do. And committees need justification. Your business case becomes the internal sales tool your champion uses when you're not in the room. It turns your product from "interesting" to "essential" by showing exactly *why* it matters to each person involved, from end users to the CFO. Without it, your deal becomes just a "nice to have" and gets stuck in no-decision land.

How to Build a Business Case:

- **Start with the pain.** What problem are you solving, and for whom? Be specific.

- **Quantify the impact.** Ask: *How much time, money, or opportunity is this costing you today?* Let them give you the numbers.

- **Translate pain into value.** Show how your solution reduces that cost or increases that gain. Use their math, not your marketing slide.

- **Tie to company goals.** Align your impact with strategic priorities, revenue targets, cost control, compliance, etc.

- **Summarize visually.** Create a clear one-pager with bullet points per stakeholder, a value breakdown, and a simple ROI snapshot.

Example: A rep selling a customer support platform learned that the buyer's current system required three full-time agents just to manage escalations. After discovering this, the rep built a summary showing:

- **Ops Leader:** Automates 60% of escalations, saving ~120 agent hours/month

- **CFO:** Annual cost savings of $85K

- **IT:** Minimal lift, integrates with existing systems
- **COO:** Improves customer response time by 35%, tied to CSAT goals
- The rep packaged this into a clean visual and added it to the Mutual Action Plan. The CFO signed off within days, because the business case answered the "why now" without needing another meeting.

HOW TO BUILD A BUSINESS CASE

Start with the pain	What problem are you solving, and for whom? Be specific.
Quantify the impact	Ask: "How much time, money, or opportunity is this costing you today?" Let them give you the numbers.
Translate pain into value	Show how your solution reduces that cost or increases that gain. Use their math, not your marketing slide.
Tie it to company goals	Align your impact with strategic priorities-revenue targets, cost control, compliance, etc.
Summarize visually	Create a clear one-pager with bullet points per stakeholder, a value breakdown, and a simple ROI snapshot
Pro Tip: Use AI tools like ChatGPT to help draft value statements, summarize stakeholder goals, or generate ROI formulas based on inputs from your calls.	

Follow this guide to build a winning business case that drives urgency and buy-in.

Pro Tip: Use AI tools like ChatGPT to help draft value statements, summarize stakeholder goals, or even generate ROI formulas based on inputs from your calls. Then plug this into a visual slide or document. Keep it simple. No fluff, just pain, impact, value, and outcomes. Include it in your deal folder, CRM, or Mutual Action Plan for full visibility.

Then share the Alignment Summary with your champion and other key stakeholders. Continue to use the details from the business case to consistently drive home your value during calls, in emails and presentations.

Even with a solid business case, objections are coming. That's not a sign of trouble, it's a buying signal. Great sellers don't wait for objections to show up, they set them up and knock them down on their terms. Let's dig into how.

Play 7: The Objection Set-Up Play

What: Proactively surface common concerns by saying: *With other clients in a similar role, some typical questions or concerns that come up are X, Y, and Z. Do any of those resonate with you?* You can also add a slide titled "What We Typically Hear" to your deck with 2 or 3 key objections and how you address them.

Why: This disarms hidden objections before they stall your deal. It shows you're experienced, confident, and prepared, not caught off guard. Buyers appreciate when you bring up tough topics first, it builds trust and positions you as a partner, not a pitch machine.

Example: You're presenting to a VP of Client Success when you pause mid-presentation: *At this stage, most leaders I speak with ask about integration* *complexity, internal adoption, or timing. Are any of those on your radar?*

The VP nods: *Yeah, the adoption part worries me.*

Boom, you've surfaced the real friction and you now have a clear path to address it.

Pro Tip: Don't sugarcoat it. Bring the real objections that actually kill deals, budget red tape, tool fatigue, resistance from the ops team. The goal is to show you've been here before and know how to navigate the minefield.

By now, you've built momentum, deepened stakeholder engagement, and positioned your solution as a strategic win. But remember, momentum doesn't guarantee a win. Execution in the Green Zone sets the stage, but it's how you close that separates the elite from the average. Before we move into the Red Zone, let's recap the key plays that keep deals moving forward.

Chapter Recap

- Momentum wins. Without movement, deals stall.
- Micro-commitments (next meetings, mutual plans, recaps) keep the drive alive.
- Single-threaded = deal risk. Multi-threading gives you internal traction and protection.
- The business case is your silent salesperson, build it clearly, tie it to KPIs, and equip your champion.
- Objections don't derail deals, surprise objections do.
- Great sellers raise potential concerns *before* the buyer does.
- Preemptive transparency builds credibility and keeps momentum moving.

Red Zone Drills:

Drill 1: Commitment Check

Review your top 5 open deals. Do all of them have a scheduled next step on the calendar? If not, reach out today and lock this in.

Drill 2: Business Case Canvas

Pick one live deal and write a 3-slide business case:

- Problem and business impact
- Your solution and value
- Expected outcome and timeline.

Review this with your champion and adjust based on their feedback.

Drill 3: Prepare a Trial Close

Choose 3 active deals and prepare one trial close question for each of the following categories:

- Value alignment:

    Based on what we've discussed so far, does this feel like it could solve the challenge you described?

- Process clarity:

    If we were to move forward, what steps would follow on your side?

- Decision readiness:

    If we're able to meet your timeline and deliver what we've outlined, would you feel confident moving forward?

You've moved the ball methodically, built consensus, and kept momentum alive through the messy middle. But now you're in the final stretch, the Red Zone, where deals are won or lost. This is where urgency tightens, objections surface, and every detail matters. The finish line is in sight, but getting across it will require precision, control, and a closer's mindset.

In the next chapter, we'll break down how to execute under pressure and close like a pro.

Get access to the Red Zone Selling Resource Center including templates, scripts, and playbooks at redzoneselling.co.

CHAPTER 4

Red Zone

The Closing Zone

Running back Marshawn Lynch, better known as Beast Mode, was a force of nature.

With a running style fueled by violence, grit, and pure will, he became one of the most feared goal-line running backs in NFL history. His legendary 67-yard touchdown run in the 2010–11 playoffs, where he broke nine tackles and sent defenders flying, became known as the "Beast Quake." It wasn't just a highlight, it was a mindset. Lynch didn't dance. He didn't hesitate. He hit the hole, ran through contact, and got the job done.

But the most infamous play involving Lynch wasn't one where he carried the ball.

It was one where he didn't.

Super Bowl XLIX. The Seattle Seahawks were down by four. Twenty-six seconds on the clock. One timeout remaining. They had the ball at the one-yard line, and Marshawn Lynch, the most dominant short-yardage runner in the league, was in the backfield.

Everyone watching knew what should happen. Hand it to Beast Mode. Let him do what he does. Power into the end zone and walk away with back-to-back championships.

But that's not what happened.

Instead, quarterback Russell Wilson dropped back and threw a slant pass into tight coverage. The ball was picked off by Patriots cornerback Malcolm Butler. Interception. Game over. Title lost.

It wasn't a bad play because of the throw. It was a bad play because it ignored the highest-percentage path to victory. The pressure of the moment got in their heads. They overcomplicated the situation when simplicity would've won.

After the game, Wilson defended the decision: *We thought we had them... I thought it was going to be a touchdown when I threw it.*

But in the Red Zone, thinking and knowing are two very different things.

That's the danger. You've done everything right to get to this point. You've qualified the opportunity, built momentum, aligned stakeholders, and now the end zone is right in front of you. But under pressure, even the best teams can overthink, over-engineer, or try to get cute with the win.

Great closers don't do that.

They don't freeze. They don't gamble. And they sure as hell don't throw slants into triple coverage when Beast Mode is behind them.

Great closers trust the process. They focus on execution. They run the high-percentage play and finish.

That's what this chapter is all about, performing under pressure, removing friction, and closing with clarity and control when it matters most. Because in the Red Zone, there's no room for hesitation. You don't hope for a win, you execute for one.

As Michael Jordan once said: *Some people want it to happen, some wish it would happen, others make it happen.*[1]

---

[1] Jordan, Michael. *Some people want it to happen, some wish it would happen, others make it happen.* Widely attributed. Used in motivational campaigns and public profiles.

The best sales pros? They make it happen.

Let's break down how to do exactly that when the end zone is in reach.

Remove the Friction – Eliminate Closing Roadblocks

In the Red Zone, everything tightens: time, attention, and scrutiny. This is where your deal is either lost in the shuffle, or pushed across the line. And often, the difference comes down to one thing: friction.

Whether it's procurement, legal, security, or finance, internal roadblocks are rarely surprises. Yet, reps often get blindsided by them because they assumed the path to close would stay smooth.

I'll never forget one deal we had with a large financial services firm. It was one of those high-stakes, high-visibility opportunities, the kind that shows up in board decks and quarterly revenue forecasts. We'd done everything right up to that point. Qualification was tight. Our champion was strong. The business case was solid, and we had multi-threaded deep into the organization. We were firmly in the Red Zone, maybe inside the five-yard line.

Then came the stall.

Legal.

They hit us with a 13-page redline to the master services agreement (MSA), some of it fair, most of it unnecessary. The issue? Their legal team didn't understand our product or our business model, and they were applying outdated compliance requirements that didn't even apply to our solution. Worse, our internal legal team was already slammed with end-of-quarter volume. Days started slipping. Emails slowed. The deal that felt like a guaranteed close suddenly had a question mark next to it in the CRM.

And then came the real gut punch: Our champion went dark.

No replies. No updates. Total silence.

It would've been easy to panic. But I'd been in the Red Zone before. I knew what this was: friction, not finality. The deal wasn't dead, it was clogged. And my job was to clear the lane.

First, I worked internally to escalate and resource our legal team. I framed the deal not just by contract value, but by strategic importance. I got the right people on our side moving.

Then I re-engaged the champion, but not with a "just checking in" email. I sent a short, bulletproof summary of everything on which we were aligned: the business pain, the outcomes, the internal support we'd already gathered. I reminded them why we were here.

That got a response. A quick one. Turns out, she hadn't gone dark, she'd been pulled into a leadership offsite and was buried. She was still in. But she needed help pushing Legal to prioritize the deal.

So we tag-teamed it. I gave her a checklist of where our legal team had already compromised. She took it directly to their general council and cut through the internal gridlock. Two weeks later, after several legal calls, we got the signed contract.

The lesson? Deals don't just die in the Red Zone, they get stuck. And if you don't stay calm, remain proactive, and lead your team through the mess, you'll lose, to friction, not the competition.

When pressure mounts, great closers don't flinch. They execute. They lead. And they finish.

In the Red Zone, your job isn't just to keep selling. It's to clear the runway for the decision to happen.

Why It Matters: A deal that hits legal at the end of the quarter is rarely going to close on time. When you're caught off guard by friction, you're reacting, not leading. And that's when urgency fades and competitors creep back in.

Elite sellers de-risk the close by identifying friction early and proactively removing it. That's why elite sellers don't wait for surprises, they anticipate them. The Obstacle Forecast Play is your first move in the Red Zone, helping you surface hidden blockers before they show up on fourth down.

Play 1: The Obstacle Forecast Play

What: Ask your champion: *What steps are left between now and signature, and who or what could potentially slow things down?*

Why: This question uncovers hidden blockers, red tape, or last-minute curveballs before they derail your close. In the Red Zone, you can't afford surprises. By forecasting friction points early, you stay in control and buy yourself time to handle issues proactively, not reactively.

Example: A rep closing a mid-size SaaS deal asked this during the final demo. The champion mentioned that legal typically insists on using their own MSA, which could add a week to the process. The rep sent over their MSA for pre-review that same day. When pricing was finalized, Legal was already in motion, saving them seven days and a fire drill.

Pro Tip: Ask specifically about Legal: *Will your legal team want us to sign your MSA, or are they open to reviewing ours?* If they prefer their own document, get a copy early. If they're flexible, send yours right away. Either way, the key is getting Legal involved *before* you finalize commercial terms, not after.

Once you've identified potential blockers, the next move is activating your champion to help clear the path. You can't close from the outside, you need an insider running point.

Play 2: The Internal Ally Activation Play

What: Activate your champion as a true internal quarterback. That means co-owning critical tasks like submitting documents to legal, chasing internal approvals, and coordinating with procurement. Support them by sharing a customized Readiness Checklist upfront, covering typical Red Zone blockers like the MSA, DPA, redlines, and payment terms.

Why: Deals stall when you're the only one pushing from the outside. In the Red Zone, you need someone inside the building keeping the momentum alive. This play creates shared ownership and turns your champion into a closer, not just a cheerleader. By laying out what's coming, you reduce friction, prevent delays, and make it easier for them to move fast.

Example: Before entering final review, a rep sent their champion a Readiness Checklist: Legal contact info, MSA status, procurement workflow, security requirements. The champion used it to chase down loose ends internally, saving time, clearing blockers early, and signaling to leadership that the deal was being run with precision.

Pro Tip: Use your Mutual Action Plan as the foundation and tie internal tasks directly to it. Then preload the friction: send the checklist before the buyer hits "approval mode." You'll look proactive, not pushy. This isn't about pressure. It's about making progress easy.

With your champion activated and blockers in motion, it's time to turn up the urgency, not with pressure, but with perspective. The best way to do that? Make the cost of inaction crystal clear.

Play 3: The Friction Preload Play

What: Use a three-pronged approach to create urgency that aligns with the buyer's reality, not your quota.

- **Time-Based Urgency:** Ask: *If you delay this until next quarter, what's the impact on your business or team?*

- **Value-Based Urgency:** Map out the value timeline: *If you want [result] by [Q4], we need to implement by [Q2], which means closing by [Q1].*

- **ROI-Based Urgency:** Frame the delay as financial loss: *If this saves $10K/month, waiting 60 days costs you $20K.*

Why: Real urgency is built on outcomes and opportunity cost, not end-of-quarter pressure. When buyers see how delay impacts *their* goals, progress, and financials, they move faster and with more conviction. This strategy flips the frame from, *We want this deal* to *You're losing by waiting.*

Example: A rep selling a hiring platform asked: *What's the cost of pushing this hiring delay another 60 days?* The VP replied that their team was burning out and they were losing candidates weekly. The rep built a value timeline that showed if they wanted new hires by September, implementation had to start by June. That clarity moved the deal from a stalled *Maybe* to a committed *Let's go.*

Pro Tip: Anchor urgency to *their* timeline, not your own. Don't say: *We'd love to get this wrapped by the end of the month.* Instead, say: *Based on your Q3 goals, we need to move now to stay on track.* Time, value, and ROI work best together, use all three to create a closing rhythm they can't ignore.

Once urgency is clear, the next step is simple, lead the buyer forward. This is where confident, assumption-based closing comes into play.

Play 4: The Confident Close Play

What: Close the deal by combining clarity with forward motion. Start with a confident statement such as: *Based on everything we've covered, let's move forward.* Then immediately shift focus to what happens next, outline the post-signature roadmap: kickoff, onboarding, timeline, and outcomes.

Why: Buyers hesitate when they feel pressure or ambiguity. This play removes both. Framing the close as the logical next step shows leadership and confidence. And by immediately focusing on post-signature execution, you redirect attention from the transaction to the transformation, what they actually care about.

Example: A rep wrapped up a pricing call by saying: *It sounds like we're aligned on everything. Let's lock this in so we can kick off implementation next Tuesday. First step is a 30-minute onboarding call with your team, sound good?*

The buyer agreed on the spot. No awkward ask, no resistance, just forward motion.

Pro Tip: Use assumptive language without being pushy: *Let's get this wrapped up so we stay on track for your Q2 rollout.* When you act like the deal is already done, buyers follow your lead, because confident execution builds trust at the finish line.

Even with strong momentum, objections can still surface late. The key isn't avoiding them, it's catching them calmly and handling them like a closer.

Play 5: The Calm Objection Catch Play

What: When a last-minute objection shows up, pricing, timing, risk, don't flinch. Acknowledge it calmly, ask a clarifying question, and reframe it with a confident response. Say something like: *Totally fair point. Let me share how we've handled that with other clients in a similar spot.*

Why: Objections in the Red Zone aren't red flags, they're buying signals. But how you respond determines whether you keep control or lose momentum. Calmly catching the objection shows leadership, keeps emotions in check, and turns potential derailments into trust-building moments.

Example: A buyer raised a concern late in the deal: *We're not sure Legal will sign off in time.* The rep responded: *Good callout, others have faced the same crunch. Here's how we've worked with legal teams to accelerate that review.*

The buyer felt heard, and the rep regained control by offering a solution, not pushing back.

Pro Tip: Have objection responses pre-loaded for the most common last-minute concerns, budget, timing, Legal, and risk. But always lead with empathy, not a rebuttal. Calm energy in the closing stretch builds trust and keeps the deal moving forward.

After handling objections with calm control, it's time to shift the focus back to action and progress. Getting personal can be the edge that keeps the deal moving.

Play 6: Get Personal

What: Build deeper relationships with your champion and key stakeholders by connecting on personal channels like SMS, WhatsApp, or even LinkedIn DMs, outside of formal company channels.

Why: Buyers tend to be more candid and responsive when they're not on email threads or recorded Zoom calls. Personal communication channels create space for real talk, whether it's a quick check-in, a subtle nudge, or celebrating a win. It's less formal, more human, and often the fastest way to get real answers.

Example: A rep had a champion who started going dark during legal review. Instead of chasing with another email, the rep sent a quick WhatsApp message: *Hey, any movement on your end? Let me know if you need anything to help keep things moving.* The champion responded immediately with an update and helped get things unstuck.

Pro Tip: Don't wait until the Red Zone to message like a human. Look for natural moments earlier in the deal: *Congrats on the promotion!* Or: *Saw your team crushed it this weekend,* to break the ice. By the time the deal gets tight, you've earned the right to text, not just email.

With relationships solid and momentum high, the final step is making sure there are no surprises at the finish line. That's where the No-Surprise Final Call comes in.

Play 7: The No-Surprise Final Call

What: Schedule one final pre-signature call with your champion (or key stakeholders) to walk through every detail before signature, pricing, legal, billing, onboarding, so there are zero surprises when the deal hits the finish line.

Why: Most last-minute delays come from overlooked details. The No-Surprise Final Call acts as a pre-flight checklist, ensuring every box is ticked, every stakeholder is aligned, and the close is clean. It prevents eleventh-hour objections by addressing them proactively, not reactively.

Example: Before a scheduled contract signing, a rep booked a 20-minute "final walkthrough" call with their champion. Together, they reviewed legal redlines, payment terms, rollout dates, and stakeholder commitments. On the signing day, the agreement went through in under an hour, no questions, no stalls, just a done deal.

You've done the hard work, anticipated blockers, activated champions, created urgency, and guided the deal with confidence. Now let's lock it in. Before we close out the Red Zone, here's a quick recap of the plays that help you finish strong.

Chapter Recap:

- The Red Zone isn't the time to get fancy, it's the time to execute.
- Identify and remove friction before it derails your close.
- Constructive urgency is rooted in the buyer's outcomes, not your deadlines.
- Great closers assume the win and lead the buyer with calm, confident direction.
- Get personal and start messaging.

Red Zone Drills:

Drill 1: Friction Forecast

For your top 3 deals, list potential blockers: Legal, Procurement, internal approvals. Write a mitigation step for each and review with your champion.

Drill 2: Buyer-Driven Timeline

Work backward from your buyer's desired outcome date. Map the deal milestones and share the timeline to create urgency based on value, not pressure.

Drill 3: Close Conversation Roleplay

Practice delivering a confident, assumptive close: *Based on everything we've covered, here's the next step. . . .* Record yourself or roleplay with a teammate.

Drill 4: Start Messaging

Review your top 5 deals and start communicating via SMS or WhatsApp in a natural way. Don't get creepy.

You've learned how to finish strong, how to remove friction, create urgency, and lead with confidence in the Red Zone. But no matter how tight your game plan is, there's one constant that can't be ignored: The defense always has a say. Competitors, internal politics, hidden objections, they don't disappear just because you're close to the goal line.

In the next chapter, we'll break down how to read the defense, spot shifting dynamics, and adjust your strategy in real time to stay in control.

Get access to the Red Zone Selling Resource Center including templates, scripts, and playbooks at redzoneselling.co.

CHAPTER 5

Reading the Defense

The Adjust and Win Zone!

Omaha, Omaha, Omaha! Ever wonder why Peyton Manning used that word at the line of scrimmage before running a play? It wasn't just for show, it was a trigger word, a last-second adjustment based on what he saw in the defense. "Omaha" could signal a change in snap count, a shift in blocking assignments, or an entirely different play. Manning's ability to read the field and adapt in real time made him one of the best quarterbacks at calling audibles.

Great salespeople operate the same way. You can't just run the same play every time and expect to win. Deals are dynamic, with competitors, decision-makers, and internal politics constantly shifting. If you're not scanning the field and making adjustments, you'll get blindsided. Success in sales requires real-time awareness, strategic pivots, and knowing when to change the call.

That starts with understanding the competition. If you don't know what you're up against, you can't properly adjust your game plan. In the next section, we'll break down how to analyze your competitors, spot their weaknesses, and position yourself for the win.

As legendary NFL coach Bill Belichick said: *Take what the defense gives you.*[2]

This chapter is about developing that quarterback mentality, reading the defense, seeing what others miss, and calling the audible when the play breaks down.

Analyze the Competition – Know What You're Up Against

You're never selling in isolation. There's always a competitor, whether it's another vendor, a homegrown tool, or the default decision to do nothing at all. You can't win if you don't know what you're up against.

Great sellers don't just focus on their own strengths. They take the time to understand their competition, how they sell, how they position, and where they fall short. When you know the defense, you know how to beat it.

I had a deal with a global media company that came down to a competitive shootout. We were up against a long-time incumbent who had the inside track and plenty of history with the client. At face value, they looked like the safer choice. But I knew from prior cycles that this company had a reputation for overpromising and under-delivering on post-sale support. Their roadmap hadn't evolved much, and their customer success team was overloaded.

Instead of pitching harder, I went into investigative mode. I reviewed previous win/loss notes, talked to sellers who had lost to this vendor, and asked our internal customer success team for patterns. I even pulled comments from public review sites that echoed what we were hearing behind closed doors.

When I met with the buying team, I didn't go negative, I went surgical. I asked: *How important is onboarding support*

---

[2] Common coaching maxim attributed to Bill Belichick and widely used in football strategy. Frequently cited in press conferences and NFL analysis.

in your first 60 days? What level of flexibility do you need if your priorities shift mid-implementation? Those questions exposed real doubts they already had about the competitor's ability to deliver.

That opened the door for me to lean into our strengths: our agility, our hands-on support model, and our track record of fast ramp-ups. By the time we reached final negotiations, we weren't just neck-and-neck, we were clearly in control of the narrative. We won the deal not by outselling, but by out-positioning the competition with precision.

That's the value of reading the defense. You don't just react, you anticipate, adjust, and attack.

Play 1: Competitive Gap Mapping

What: Map your product or service side-by-side with your top competitors. This includes features, pricing, onboarding experience, customer success model, roadmap flexibility, and market reputation. The goal is to identify where you outperform, where you're vulnerable, and where the gaps in their armor give you a chance to strike.

Why: You can't win if you don't know the defense. Deals are rarely lost because the competitor is better, it's because the seller didn't effectively *differentiate*. When you understand your opponent's weaknesses better than they do, you don't have to outsell, you out-position. This is where top closers shine.

Example: In a competitive bake-off with a global media company, I went deep on a legacy competitor. I reviewed win/loss notes, sourced internal feedback, and combed through online reviews. The result? I uncovered consistent gaps in post-sale support and product agility. Instead of going negative, I asked such targeted questions as: *What's your ideal onboarding experience in the first 60 days?* That prompted the buying team to reflect on a known weakness, without me ever calling it out directly. I then leaned into our agility and support, shifting the entire narrative in our favor. We won by playing chess, not checkers.

Pro Tip: Don't wait for late-stage pressure to do this work. Build a competitive gap map as early as the Yellow Zone, then refine it as you gather intel throughout the deal cycle.

Bonus: Share a version of the MAP with your champion, it gives them ammo to sell *you* internally while planting doubt about the competition.

Play 2: Win/Loss Autopsy

What: Break down your last five deals, both wins and losses, to uncover the real reasons behind the outcome. Focus specifically on competitive dynamics: What did the other vendor do well? Where did they fall short? What objections surfaced, and how did you handle (or fumble) them? This is your game film. Study it like a coach reviewing Sunday tape.

Why: Patterns don't lie. Top performers don't just move on after a win or loss, they extract insights and sharpen their edge. Understanding how competitors beat you, or how you beat them, helps you spot red flags sooner, position more effectively, and come into the next deal better prepared. You don't just get better by doing; you get better by reviewing.

Example: After losing a major deal to a newer player in the space, we ran a post-mortem. We discovered they had leaned hard into executive relationships early, while we focused on the mid-level. That insight changed how we opened my next few deals. We multi-threaded earlier, booked time with VPs sooner, and re-positioned our value for a strategic audience. Result? A win in the next two competitive head-to-heads against the same vendor.

Pro Tip: Don't wait until year-end to do this. Schedule a 30-minute "autopsy" within 72 hours of every major deal closing, win or lose. Include reps, sales engineers, and even customer success.

Bonus move: Ask your buyer for a quick "why we chose you" or "why we didn't" recap. Their answers often reveal more than internal speculation ever could.

Play 3: Real-World Buyer Intel

What: Ask your prospects directly what other solutions they're evaluating, and what stands out to them about each one. Then, go deeper. Use follow-up questions to surface hidden preferences, concerns, or friction points. This isn't about fishing for gossip, it's about getting the raw truth on how you stack up in the buyer's mind *right now*.

Why: Most reps stop at *We're looking at a few options* and move on. Elite sellers know that *what the buyer says* and *what they believe* are often two different things. By staying curious and non-defensive, you uncover where the real decision criteria live. And once you understand their mental scoreboard, you can reposition and win before the final whistle.

Example: I was mid-cycle with a CFO who mentioned they were also looking at two competitors. Instead of glossing over it, I leaned in: *Interesting.*

Out of curiosity, what stands out to you about each option so far?

His response gave me two gold nuggets: He liked their dashboards but was concerned about data delays. I followed up with: *How critical is real-time accuracy for your reporting cadence?*

That opened a door to anchor our value proposition directly to his top priority, and plant doubt about the other alternatives. He didn't realize he'd tipped his hand, but it was all I needed to pivot and win the deal.

Pro Tip: Make this part of your standard discovery script, not just a one-off move. Ask:

- *What are you seeing from other vendors that you like?*

- *Is there anything you wish you could combine from the different solutions?*

- *What one thing are you're unsure about with any of the options?*

These open up a goldmine of buyer psychology, and once it's out in the open, you can reshape the narrative in your favor.

Gather Competitive Intelligence – See the Full Picture

Great sellers don't rely on a single source of truth. They gather intelligence from every possible channel, filter out the noise, and spot the real patterns. The sharper your visibility into the competitive landscape, the better your positioning, and the faster you can adapt.

The most effective way to organize all this insight is with a simple but powerful framework: the SWOT analysis.

A SWOT analysis breaks your competitive intel into four buckets, Strengths, Weaknesses, Opportunities, and Threats:

- **Strengths** are what your competitor does well, product features, pricing flexibility, brand recognition, or support depth.

- **Weaknesses** highlight where they struggle, slow implementation, gaps in functionality, poor customer service, or inconsistent results.

- **Opportunities** represent market trends or company situations you can exploit, leadership turnover, product stagnation, or poor fit in a specific vertical.

- **Threats** are areas where they might outmaneuver you, aggressive discounting, strategic partnerships, or faster roadmap execution.

SWOT ANALYSIS

STRENGTHS

Strengths include areas where your competitor excels, such as strong brand recognition, advanced features, value pricing, or an established customer base.

WEAKNESSES

Weaknesses reveal their shortcomings, such as pricing limitations, poor customer support, implementation challenges, or gaps in their product offering.

OPPORTUNITIES

Opportunities highlight market shifts, trends, or gaps that you can take advantage of, such as a competitor struggling in a specific industry.

THREATS

Threats represent challenges that could impact your ability to compete, including aggressive pricing strategies, strategic partnerships, or rapid innovation from rivals.

Use a SWOT analysis to identify strengths, weaknesses, opportunities, and threats that impact your deal strategy.

By organizing your findings into this framework, you create a clear picture of where to attack, how to defend, and where to focus your positioning.

Play 4: The Multi-Channel Intel Sweep

What: Gather real-time intel on your competitors and prospects by scanning multiple public channels. Dig into G2, TrustRadius, Reddit threads, LinkedIn updates, Glassdoor reviews, press releases, product pages, customer testimonials, and analyst reports. Look for patterns, recurring praise, consistent complaints, positioning gaps, or market messaging changes. Then use those insights to shape your questions and sharpen your pitch.

Why: One source is a data point. Multiple sources create a strategic pattern. Most reps glance at a LinkedIn profile and call it research. Great sellers create an intel stack. This lets you speak with credibility, tailor your message, and ask questions that show you're two steps ahead of the competition. It also helps you identify soft spots your competitors hope buyers won't notice.

Example: Before a pitch to a fintech prospect, we ran a quick intel sweep on their top vendor. On G2, several reviews praised their user interface, but complained about integration speed. Their VP of Product had recently posted about needing better API flexibility. Their website didn't mention implementation timelines, another red flag. During our call, we casually asked: *How critical is integration agility for your team's roadmap?* That one question exposed a major pain point. We won that deal by anchoring on speed and flexibility, and backed it up with customer stories that hit those exact themes.

Pro Tip: Use LinkedIn Sales Navigator to follow key accounts, execs, and competitors. You'll get daily updates on job changes, posts, and company growth. For a budget move, set Google Alerts on company names, competitors, and such keywords as **"[Competitor] + implementation"** or **"Customer experience + [Vendor Name]"** to get insights delivered right to your inbox. That's free intel working 24/7.

Play 5: The AI Assist

What: Leverage AI tools like Crayon, Klue, NotebookLM, or ChatGPT to rapidly analyze competitor activity at scale. These tools can surface product changes, messaging shifts, sentiment trends, pricing moves, and even hiring patterns, giving you a real-time edge without spending hours buried in research.

Why: AI multiplies your effort. While traditional research is slow and surface-level, AI tools help you spot hidden competitive angles, compress research time, and uncover themes that would otherwise be missed. It's not just about doing more, it's about seeing more and acting faster than your competition. Every day you're not using AI, your rivals might be.

Example: I had a strategic pitch coming up against a fast-moving startup competitor. Instead of combing through their site manually, I used Crayon to track their website changes over the last 60 days and noticed they had removed references to a key feature, suggesting it was being deprecated. I then ran their G2 reviews through ChatGPT and asked for recurring concerns. Integration delays and lack of onboarding support came up repeatedly. Armed with that intel, I built questions that exposed their soft spots without ever going negative. That edge helped me steer the conversation, and the deal, our way.

Pro Tip: Use ChatGPT to analyze public reviews or transcripts. Try this prompt:

Summarize the most common strengths and weaknesses mentioned in these reviews for [Competitor].

You can also feed the tool a competitor's blog content or press releases and ask:

"What trends or positioning shifts do you notice over the past 6 months?"

Boom! Instant strategic insight without the manual grind.

Play 6: Build Your Own Battle Card

What: Create a dynamic, deal-ready battle card for each of your top competitors. This isn't a dusty slide deck. It's a concise, up-to-date document your team uses before key calls. It should include:

- The competitor's core messaging and positioning.
- Go-to objections they are known to plant.
- Pricing structure and discounting tactics.
- Product strengths and known gaps.
- Sales tactics (land and expand, discount plays, speed-to-POC).
- Support and implementation issues (if any).

Why: Deals are won in the details. A solid battle card ensures your intel turns into action, in discovery, during objection handling, and especially in competitive bake-offs. Instead of reacting mid-call, your team walks in prepared to out-position and out-execute.

Example: My team was in a three-way shootout with two aggressive competitors. Before a key call, they reviewed our internal battle card, which included one rival's known tendency to offer early-stage discounts in exchange for long-term contracts, something that had burned prospects in the past.

When the buyer mentioned that competitor's "aggressive pricing," a rep leaned in: *Are they offering any discount-based commitments up front?*

That prompted a pause, and concern. The prospect circled back two days later, asking if we could provide more flexible terms. Our team stayed above the discount war and won on trust, flexibility, and readiness.

Pro Tip: Make battle cards a team sport. Build them collaboratively with sales, marketing, product, and customer success. Everyone brings different intel. Use tools like Google Docs or Notion for version control and accessibility. Keep it clean, visual, and actionable. And don't forget to add "Counter Questions", smart, open-ended prompts your reps can use to reframe the conversation and expose weaknesses without going negative. This is another great task where AI can be quite helpful.

Play 7: Translate SWOT to Strategy

What: Don't let your SWOT analysis sit on a slide collecting dust. Use it to shape your positioning in real time. For every competitor strength, have a countermove. For every weakness, craft a value prop. For every threat, develop a risk-reduction play. Turn static intel into dynamic messaging that resonates with your buyer's priorities.

Why: Insight is only valuable when it drives action. Most sellers do the analysis but stop short of using it to reframe the conversation and control the narrative. When you apply SWOT to your pitch, discovery questions, and objection handling, you're no longer reacting, you're steering.

Example: My team was going up against a lower-cost competitor known for fast pilots. Their pricing was hard to beat, so instead of trying to match them, we pivoted. We used our SWOT to highlight long-term ROI, pointing out their history of needing costly custom work later. We asked: *Are you optimizing for initial cost, or total success over 12 months?* That reframed the decision, shifted the buyer's lens, and helped us justify a premium position. SWOT wasn't just a framework, it became our strategic weapon.

Pro Tip: Don't just analyze the competition, SWOT your own team. Know where you're strong, where you're vulnerable, and where your execution shines. That self-awareness gives your messaging credibility and helps your team navigate around traps instead of falling into them.

Bonus: Use the battle card format to build in SWOT as a quick-hit reference field.

Every deal has defenders, and not all of them wear name tags. These are the hidden stakeholders who don't show up on your calls but have the power to slow-roll, stall, or kill your deal behind the scenes.

If you don't find them early, you'll learn about them the hard way. This section is about spotting resistance before it becomes a redline. It's time to read the defense and play the internal game like a pro.

Play 8: The Stakeholder Map Audit

What: Review and update your stakeholder map mid-deal to make sure you have full coverage across all key roles: Champion, Executive Sponsor, Economic Buyer, Technical Buyer, Evaluators, Procurement, Legal, and yes, Gatekeepers. Identify who's actively engaged, who's missing, and where hidden resistance might live.

Why: Deals get stuck when you miss including someone critical, or worse, when an unseen player blocks you late in the game. A stakeholder map audit helps you spot gaps before they become problems. If you're not multi-threaded and aligned across the full buying committee, you're flying blind, and that's how you lose winnable deals.

Example: Midway through a six-figure SaaS deal, a rep conducted a Stakeholder Map Audit and realized they hadn't engaged Procurement or the CIO yet, the two groups that had blocked deals in the past. The rep worked with the champion to secure early introductions, addressed their concerns proactively, and kept the deal moving smoothly through final approvals.

Pro Tip: Specifically ask: *Is there anyone who controls access, signs off on vendors, or could slow this down later?* Gatekeepers, which might be procurement leads, IT admins, or legal reviewers, often lurk behind the scenes until it's too late. Engage them early with respect and a spirit of partnership, not avoidance.

STAKEHOLDER MAP AUDIT

Stakeholder Role	Engaged	Missing
Champion		
Executive Sponsor		
Economic Buyer		
Technical Buyer		
Evaluators		
Procurement		
Legal		

Use the stakeholder map audit to assess engagement levels and uncover gaps in deal coverage.

Once you've mapped the full field, the next move is to dig deeper. Knowing who's involved is good, knowing who might resist is even better. Let's uncover potential blockers before they become real problems.

Play 9: The Deal Blocker Discovery

What: Schedule a strategic call with your champion to explore potential internal blockers. Ask direct, non-threatening questions such as: *Who might have concerns about this?* Or: *Is there anyone who could slow this down or say no?*

Why: Every deal has a defender, someone who's skeptical, risk-averse, or just misaligned. The earlier you find them, the better your chances of addressing their concerns and neutralizing their influence. If you don't ask, you'll only find out after the deal stalls, or disappears.

Example: A rep selling a data integration platform asked their champion: *Who typically challenges new tools like this?* The champion revealed that the head of security was known for slowing down approvals. The rep offered to meet with them early and preempted their concerns with a security brief, removing friction before it showed up.

Pro Tip: Position the call as a strategy session: *I want to make sure we're set up to win internally. Can we walk through who else might need to weigh in?* This makes it feel collaborative, not political. Alternatively, you can work this question into any call if done tactfully.

Bonus: Do this early in the Green Zone, and revisit it again in the Red Zone. Finding internal resistance is only part of the battle. The next threat is external, competitors still lurking in the shadows. Before you get blindsided, it's time to set the trap and surface any hidden competition.

Play 10: The Competitor Trap Play

What: Ask your champion targeted questions to detect if a competitor is still active in the deal. Use prompts like:

- *Are you evaluating anyone else for this?*
- *What does the internal feedback look like on other vendors?*

- *What would make someone internally lean toward another solution?*

Why: The worst competition is the kind you don't see coming. Many deals go dark not because of pricing or timing, but because another vendor beat you in a meeting to which you weren't invited. This play helps you flush out hidden threats so you can defend your value, sharpen your positioning, and avoid being used as column fodder.

Example: A rep nearing the finish line asked their champion: *Is there anyone still advocating for another solution?* The champion revealed that a VP of Ops had a relationship with a competing vendor. The rep quickly adjusted their strategy, armed their champion with a competitive battle card, and scheduled a head-to-head comparison meeting. That move protected the deal and ultimately won the close.

Pro Tip: Don't ask: *Are you looking at competitors?* Instead, ask *how* they're evaluating others, *who* might still be supporting them, and *what* concerns those stakeholders might have. That's how you turn invisible competition into a visible advantage.

Expose the Inefficiencies — Identify Buying Process Gaps

Most companies don't have a clean, well-oiled buying process. Even when interest is high, deals get bogged down in confusion, unclear next steps, missing stakeholders, or internal misalignment that stalls progress. It's not that buyers don't want to move forward. They just don't always know how.

That's where great sellers make their mark.

Elite reps don't just sell solutions, they bring structure to the decision-making process. They identify the friction points before they become full-blown blockers and help the buyer navigate around them.

I had a deal like this with a mid-sized tech team inside a global media company. There was real interest and strong alignment. But the deal kept stalling out, not because of objections, but because the internal process was a mess. Legal wasn't looped in. Procurement kept surfacing late. And no one was sure who had final approval authority.

At first, I assumed they were dragging their feet. But then I realized the truth, they didn't have a defined buying process. They were trying to move forward but didn't know how to coordinate internally.

So I stepped in.

I mapped out a simple buying roadmap based on what we'd seen in similar enterprise deals. It included a legal checkpoint, a procurement call, and a light ROI deck for finance. I framed it as a draft and sent it over to my champion with the subject line: *Here's a possible path, tell me what's missing.*

That one-pager created clarity. It gave them something to which they could react and customize for their situation. Within 48 hours, they'd added a few internal notes, assigned ownership to key steps, and we were back in motion. We closed the deal two weeks later, not because I sold harder, but because I helped them get out of their own way.

This is what it means to read the defense and lead through the chaos. Sometimes the biggest value you bring is not just the product, but the path to the decision.

Play 11: Decision Confidence Question

What: Ask your buyer: *Have you bought a solution like this before? What helped or hurt that process?*

This question uncovers their past experience, confidence level, internal gaps, and potential blind spots. It shifts the tone from "selling" to "guiding," and opens the door for you to lead them through the decision with confidence.

Why: Most buyers aren't experts in buying what you sell. Even seasoned execs might only make a decision like this once every few years. When you understand their level of familiarity, and where previous processes broke down, you can proactively fill the gaps, manage expectations, and reduce perceived risk. This play builds trust while subtly establishing control.

Example: One of our AEs asked this question during discovery with a VP of HR evaluating a new platform. She admitted they'd been burned before by a rushed decision with limited cross-functional input. That gave us the perfect opening to say: *We've seen that too, which is why we recommend looping in [X, Y, Z] early.* That one insight helped us guide the process, build internal alignment, and avoid the same mistake. We didn't just sell the platform, we sold decision confidence.

Pro Tip: Follow up with:

- *What would a smooth decision process look like for you this time around?*

- *Is there anything you want to do differently than last time?*

These questions elevate your role from vendor to trusted advisor, someone who's not just closing a deal but helping them navigate it smarter.

You can't beat an opponent you can't see. By reading the defense early, spotting blockers, gatekeepers, and hidden competitors, you stay a step ahead and keep control of the deal. Let's recap the key plays that protect your close.

Chapter Recap

- Analyze the competition like a quarterback would study game film.
- Gather competitive intelligence from multiple channels and AI tools.
- Conduct a SWOT analysis to identify where you can differentiate and counter.
- Find all decision-makers early to avoid stalls and surprises.
- Expose gaps in the buyer's process and guide them toward a confident, frictionless decision.

Red Zone Drills:

Drill 1: Competitive SWOT

Choose your top competitor and complete a SWOT analysis. Identify three angles to highlight your differentiation in upcoming deals.

Drill 2: Build Your Battle Card

Create or refresh your top three competitor battle cards. Include positioning, feature gaps, pricing trends, and common objections.

Drill 3: Stakeholder Map

Pick one live opportunity and build a stakeholder map. Mark who you've met and who's missing. Fill the gaps.

Drill 4: Win/Loss Reflection

Review your last five deals. For each, answer: *What did we do well against the competition? What should we have done differently?*

Now that you've identified the friction and neutralized the threats, the next challenge is keeping the momentum alive. Deals don't stall because buyers lose interest, they stall because sellers lose pace. In Chapter 6, we'll focus on how to keep deals moving without losing control.

Get access to the Red Zone Selling Resource Center including templates, scripts, and playbooks at redzoneselling.co.

Keeping Deals in Motion

Just Keep Moving

In 2004, I set a goal that seemed out of reach: I was going to run the New York City Marathon. At the time, I had never run more than a 10K. A full marathon? That was an entirely different beast. To prepare, I joined the NJ Road Runners Club, a group that provided the structure, accountability, and motivation I needed to push myself beyond my comfort zone.

My training officially kicked off in June. Over the next five months, I pounded out 20 to 35 miles per week, with grueling long runs every Sunday morning at 7 AM. Those runs stretched from 13 to 20 miles, building the endurance I would need on race day. In between, I did sprint work, recovery runs, and everything necessary to get my body and my mindset ready. By the time November rolled around, I was in the best shape of my life. I had put in the work, followed the plan, and felt ready to conquer the 26.2 miles ahead of me.

But as Mike Tyson famously said: *Everyone has a plan until they get punched in the face.*[3]

Race day arrived on November 7, 2004. The morning started at a cool 49 degrees, but by noon, the temperature had climbed to 68. That mattered a lot. My training runs had all been in cooler,

---

[3] Mike Tyson famously said this when asked how he would handle Holyfield's fight plan. It's since become a metaphor for how real-world adversity disrupts theory.

early morning conditions, and now I was dealing with unexpected heat. To make things worse, the marathon didn't start for amateur runners until 9:10 AM, and my group didn't cross the starting line until 10 AM. And we had just moved the clocks back an hour to adjust to standard time.

I started strong, fueled by adrenaline and the energy of the roaring New York City crowds. But by the halfway mark, something felt off. I was weaker than expected, drained in a way I hadn't anticipated. My body was burning through energy at a rate I hadn't anticipate in my training. By mile 18, when I saw my wife and kids cheering me on from the sidelines, I was ready to quit. I still had 8.2 miles to go, and every step felt like a battle.

At that moment, I made a simple decision: *Just keep moving.* Whether I was running, jogging, or even walking, I refused to stop. I put one foot in front of the other, pushed through the pain, and willed myself across the finish line in 4 hours, 29 minutes, and 53 seconds.

It wasn't about speed, or time, it was about finishing.

Sales is no different. Keeping deals in motion is what separates closers from those who come up short. Momentum is everything. If a deal stalls, it dies. If you keep it moving, you give yourself a chance to win.

That's what this chapter is all about.

Momentum Is a Mindset

In the Green Zone, deals don't die from lack of interest, they die from inertia. Prospects get overwhelmed. Stakeholders disappear. Priorities shift. Without clear direction, the deal flatlines.

Momentum isn't built by checking in or circling back. It's built by staying in control of the tempo, driving the next step, bringing in the right people, and reinforcing urgency.

Before we dive into specific plays to keep deals in motion, let's take a quick step back.

Most sales teams *have* a process. But is it structured to win? If your process isn't built around the 4 Pillars of a Winning Sales

Process, you're not just at risk of deals stalling, you're building on shaky ground.

The 4 Pillars of a Winning Sales Process:

- **Clear Stages:** Defined deal stages that align with how buyers make decisions.

- **Buyer-Based Milestones**: Progress is measured by *what the buyer has done*, not just what *you've done*.

- **Next-Step Discipline:** Every stage ends with a scheduled commitment to keep momentum alive.

- **Multi-Threading Strategy:** A plan to engage all key stakeholders at each stage.

This isn't about replacing what works, it's a way to *pressure-test* your process. If even one pillar is weak, momentum will suffer.

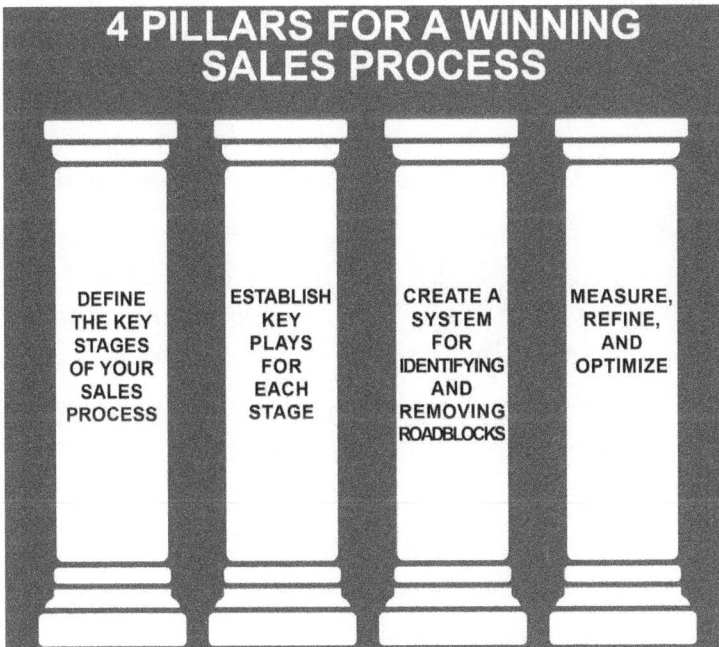

4 PILLARS FOR A WINNING SALES PROCESS

| DEFINE THE KEY STAGES OF YOUR SALES PROCESS | ESTABLISH KEY PLAYS FOR EACH STAGE | CREATE A SYSTEM FOR IDENTIFYING AND REMOVING ROADBLOCKS | MEASURE, REFINE, AND OPTIMIZE |

The 4 pillars are essential for building a winning sales process that drives consistent results.

Letting a prospect take time to think things through without an agreed-upon next step is like walking off the track mid-race. You're not pausing, you're giving up the lead.

Play 1: Close for the Next Step, Every Time

What: At the end of every sales interaction, discovery call, demo, pricing conversation, proposal review, lock in the next step before you hang up. This could be a calendar invite, stakeholder meeting, technical review, or contract walkthrough. Never leave it vague.

Why: A deal without a scheduled next step is a deal at risk. Your sales process is a chain of micro-commitments, remove one link, and the whole thing breaks. Letting a buyer "get back to you" creates open loops, missed follow-ups, and deals that quietly die. Control the cadence by guiding the next move every time.

Example: One of our reps wrapped up a killer proposal review with a VP and ended the call by saying: *Just shoot me a note once you've had a chance to review it internally.* Guess what? The deal ghosted for three weeks.

Same rep, new deal. This time, he ended with: *Let's book 30 minutes Thursday to review feedback and align on final next steps. That way we don't lose momentum.*

The VP agreed on the spot. That meeting kept the deal alive, cleared final objections, and led to a signed contract within the week. Strong close = strong control.

Pro Tip: Have 2 time slots ready before the call ends. Try this script:

What works better, Thursday at 10am or Friday at 2pm, for a quick alignment on next steps?

Add it to the calendar while you're still on the call. Don't accept: *Let me check*, just close the loop. Train your buyers to operate with momentum, not indecision.

Scheduling the next meeting is just the first move. Once the deal is rolling, you need to keep reinforcing alignment along the way.

Play 2: The Mid-Deal Recap Play

What: Send a midpoint recap that summarizes where you've been, what's been agreed to, and what's coming next. Bullet points over long paragraphs.

Why: A mid-deal check-in reduces confusion, shows leadership, and prevents stakeholders from drifting or forgetting commitments.

Example: At the halfway mark of a software evaluation, a rep sent a "Deal So Far" email outlining key decisions, timelines, and next steps. It re-engaged two stakeholders who had gone quiet and helped keep the timeline intact.

Pro Tip: Make it visual if possible, a simple timeline or checklist catches more attention than a wall of text.

Recapping progress is important, but urgency comes from tying next steps back to something bigger, the buyer's own deadlines.

Play 3: The Decision Timeline Anchor Play

What: Early in the sales cycle, ask: *When would you ideally like to have this live?* Then work backward from that goal to create urgency and shape every action item.

Why: Deadlines matter when they belong to the buyer, not the seller. Anchoring to their target keeps everyone focused and moving with purpose.

Example: During discovery, a rep learned the buyer needed to launch by Q4 to meet a revenue target. They framed every step around hitting that goal, which helped move Legal, Security, and Procurement faster than usual.

Pro Tip: Re-anchor the timeline at every major meeting: *Just as a reminder, since you want to go live by October, we'll want to finalize X by August.*

Even with a strong timeline, deals can drift if your internal advocates lose energy. Keeping your champion fired up is critical.

Play 4: The Re-Energize the Champion Play

What: Check in with your champion mid-deal and bring them something fresh: a new insight, competitive intel, updated ROI data, or a quick win.

Why: Champions get busy, distracted, or discouraged. Giving them new ammunition keeps them engaged, refocused, and actively selling your solution inside the organization.

Example: A rep sent their champion a quick case study showing how a similar client accelerated their onboarding timeline. The champion used it to re-motivate their CFO and keep the deal moving.

Pro Tip: Position the re-engagement as value for *them* personally: *Saw this and thought it might help you get faster buy-in internally.*

Keeping the champion active helps, but you also need to keep your own pulse on the deal's health as it moves forward.

Play 5: The Progress Pulse Check Play

What: Reach out with a quick check-in question such as: *How's everything feeling on your end?* Or: *Are we still tracking toward [goal]?*

Why: Small check-ins uncover small problems before they turn into big delays. It shows you're paying attention without being annoying.

Example: Two weeks after a proposal review, a rep sent a quick Slack message: *Still good to move into legal review this week?*

The champion flagged a new concern early, allowing the rep to adjust the plan without losing weeks.

Pro Tip: Use short, informal communication, Slack, text, quick DMs, to keep the tone light and easy. You're checking the weather, not launching a full forecast.

Play 6: Thread Early, Thread Deep

What: Don't put your entire deal in the hands of one person. Multi-thread by connecting with key stakeholders across departments and levels, economic buyers, technical evaluators, influencers, end users, Legal, and Procurement. Ask questions like:

- *Who else will be part of this decision?*
- *What does your internal approval path usually look like?*
- *Who owns implementation once this goes live?*

Early threading gives you insight and influence, not just access.

Why: Single-threaded deals are fragile. If your one contact goes dark, gets promoted, or pushes it down the priority list, your deal stalls, or dies. Multi-threading gives you coverage and reduces risk. Even more importantly, it builds internal consensus. The more people who are bought in, the more gravity your deal has. Multi-threading isn't just insurance, it's political capital.

Example: Our team was deep into a deal with a promising Director-level champion. But just before the final proposal review, she took emergency leave. Because we hadn't built other relationships, the deal froze. We learned the hard way. On the next opportunity, we started threading from call two, looped in the VP of Finance, the head of IT, and a senior user from the ops team. When the primary contact went quiet, the others kept pushing. We didn't just survive, we closed faster than expected.

Pro Tip: Use a Stakeholder Tracker in your deal notes or CRM.

For each contact, log:

- Name, Title, Role in the Decision
- Influence Level: High / Medium / Low
- Stance:
    - Green = Ally
    - Yellow = Unknown
    - Red = Blocker
- Last Contact Date

- Next Step to Advance Engagement

If you're still single-threaded after your second meeting, that's a red flag. Thread early. Thread deep. Win consistently.

Create Urgency Without Creating Pressure

Prospects don't move because they're interested. They move because something is at stake. When there's no urgency, good intentions fade into the background. Interest without urgency is the fastest path to a stalled deal.

I was working a deal with a mid-sized e-commerce company that had been growing quickly but struggling with operational inefficiencies. We had a strong champion, solid solution fit, and even verbal alignment from their COO. But things started to slow. Meetings pushed out. Emails took longer to get responses. The deal was losing steam.

Instead of pushing harder, I stepped back and reframed the conversation. I revisited their earlier pain points, specifically how much revenue they were losing from abandoned carts due to slow page loads and inventory sync issues. I had our team run a quick analysis and estimated they were losing over $30,000 a month from those gaps alone.

Then I sent a note: *If we move forward this month, we can have your new system live before peak selling season hits. That means fewer lost sales, faster site performance, and stronger revenue heading into Q4. Waiting even one month could mean leaving another $30K on the table.*

That shifted everything. I didn't pressure them. I clarified the impact of inaction and tied it to their own business goals. Within days, we had the final approvals, and the deal moved into procurement.

Urgency isn't about hard-selling. It's about helping the buyer prioritize progress by making the consequences of delay real and tangible.

Tie your solution to:

- Time sensitivity: *We can still hit your Q2 launch date if we move this week.*
- Cost of inaction: *This delay is costing you $30K per month in lost revenue.*
- Competitive edge: *If you're first to market with this capability, you'll set the pace for your category.*

When urgency is grounded in the customer's world, not your quota, it becomes a catalyst for action. Urgency isn't about hard-selling. It's about helping your buyer prioritize progress.

Spot the Stalls Before They Start

Deals don't usually blow up, they fade out. One week turns into two. That next step never gets scheduled. Before you know it, it's been 30 days since your last touchpoint.

The best reps don't just move deals forward, they prevent them from stalling in the first place.

Watch for these warning signs:

- The buyer asks for time to review without booking a follow-up.
- You don't know who the budget holder is.
- Multiple meetings, but no decision-makers involved.
- They say you're the top choice, but haven't pulled in their Procurement or Legal teams.

When you see the stall forming, adjust. Add urgency. Bring in a stakeholder. Reframe the value.

DEAL STALL RISK

LACK OF
URGENCY

STAKEHOLDER
SILENCE

SHIFTING
PRIORITIES

NO CLEAR
NEXT STEP

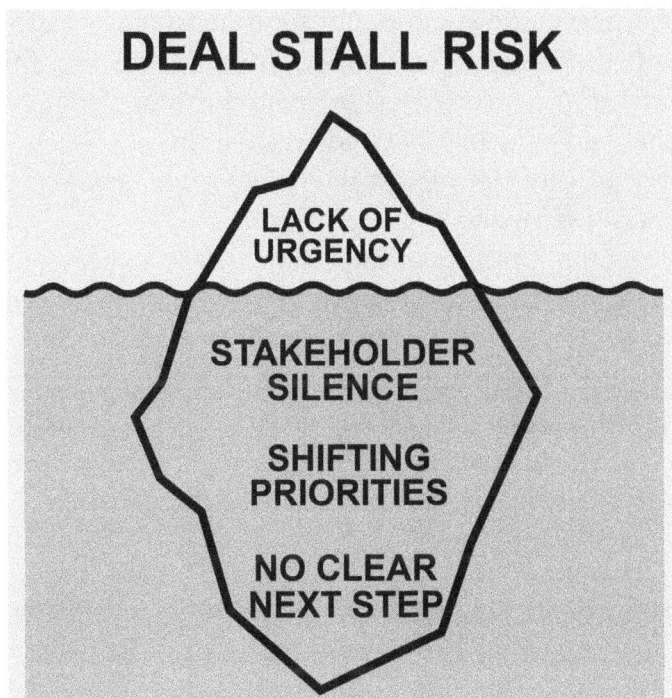

*Uncover hidden risks below the surface that can stall
your deal and derail your close.*

Reignite a Stalled Deal

A few years back, my team was working a deal with a mid-market e-commerce company that had strong momentum early on. The discovery call went great, the demo resonated, and we had verbal buy-in from the head of operations. Then, radio silence.

Weeks passed. No replies. No meetings. Nothing but an occasional out-of-office bounce-back. I could've written it off. We could've sent the typical "just checking in" email and hoped for the best.

Instead, we reframed my approach.

We went back through the notes and realized their team had mentioned launching a new digital storefront in Q2. So I built a quick one-pager showing how our solution could accelerate that launch timeline, reduce onboarding friction, and help them hit their metrics. We included a short customer story from a similar brand that had gone live fast and crushed their Q2 goals.

I hit send with the subject line: *Here's how we help you hit your Q2 launch target.*

Still nothing. Until about a week later. They finally responded, apologizing and asking to set up a call to reconnect. We got back on a call that week. Four weeks later, the deal was closed.

That's how you reignite a stalled deal. Not by hoping. By re-engaging with intent, insight, and strategy.

If a deal's gone quiet, don't just follow up. Change the energy. Change the message. Here's how to shake things up:

- **Send new info:** Don't resend old decks. Share something fresh, a relevant case study, customer stat, or recent market insight tied directly to their role or priorities.

- **Change the narrative:** *Since we last talked, I mapped out how this could support your Q2 launch plan. Let me show you.*

- **Escalate:** Loop in a new stakeholder or executive sponsor. Sometimes, deals stall because your champion lost influence or energy. Bring in a fresh voice to reset momentum.

- **Use a time-based trigger:** *If we get started this month, we can be live by [X date], but the window is tight. After that, you'll risk falling behind.*

Stalled deals don't fix themselves. You have to revive them with relevance and purpose. The more targeted your approach, the faster you'll get them moving again.

Momentum is never accidental, it's built through intentional, consistent moves. These plays keep deals from drifting and ensure you stay in the driver's seat. Before we move on, let's recap the strategies that keep your pipeline in motion.

Chapter Recap

- Momentum is everything, a stalled deal is a dying deal.

- Close for the next step every time. Don't leave a meeting without a calendar invite.

- Multi-thread your deals. More stakeholders means more stability.

- Urgency drives movement. Tie your solution to time, cost, or competitive pressure.

- Reignite slow deals with fresh angles. Don't check in, challenge, reframe, and re-engage.

- Use mutual action plans to create clarity and keep deals on track.

Red Zone Drills

Drill 1: Pipeline Audit

Pick three deals that have slowed. What's missing, urgency, time anchor, next step, or stakeholder coverage?

Drill 2: Thread Mapping

For a live opportunity, build a stakeholder map. Who's engaged? Who's missing? Fill the gaps.

Drill 3: Next-Step Challenge

Look at your last five calls. Did you book the next step before ending each one? If not, fix that going forward.

Drill 4: Build a Mutual Action Plan

Take one high-value deal and build a mutual action plan with your buyer. Use it to align internally and externally.

When the middle of the deal gets messy, your job is to lead. The best closers don't wait, they drive. Keep the deal moving, and you stay in control.

Momentum gets you to the edge of the win, but preparation is what gets you across the goal line. Keeping a deal in motion is critical, but once you enter the Red Zone, the game changes. Every detail matters. Every stakeholder must be aligned. And any misstep can cost you the deal.

You're no longer building interest. You're closing. And that requires a different mindset, a different level of discipline, and a different set of plays.

In the next chapter, we'll focus on Red Zone Readiness, how to prepare every deal for a strong finish, eliminate last-minute surprises, and execute when the pressure is highest. Because getting close isn't enough. The best reps don't just drive the ball, they finish the play.

Get access to the Red Zone Selling Resource Center including templates, scripts, and playbooks at redzoneselling.co.

CHAPTER 7

Red Zone Readiness

Execute When It Counts

Fun fact: According to the NFL, 74.6% of all touchdowns since 2010 have come from inside the Red Zone.

That's not a fluke. Teams train for those moments. They build Red Zone-specific plays, adjust for pressure, and execute with focus. Quarterbacks like Josh Allen, Lamar Jackson, and Jalen Hurts led the league in Red Zone scoring in 2024. All three made the playoffs. Jalen Hurts went to the Super Bowl and walked away as the MVP.

That's no coincidence. Quarterbacks who dominate in the Red Zone are the ones who win games. They anticipate, adjust, and execute under pressure.

Sales is no different.

Getting into the final stage of a deal doesn't guarantee a win. You have to eliminate last-minute blockers, manage internal dynamics, and close with discipline. I learned this the hard way on one of the biggest deals of my career.

While leading enterprise sales at Kustomer, I worked a deal with a global travel booking company. We were 15 months into the cycle. Everything was aligned. Verbal approvals were in. Then Procurement stepped in. Legal followed. Things slowed. The entire deal could have collapsed.

Instead of pushing or panicking, we shifted our strategy. We took a partnership approach with procurement and kept senior leadership aligned. We treated Procurement like a stakeholder, not a roadblock. It took another three months, but we stayed disciplined, navigated every step, and closed the largest deal in company history, seven figures, just before year-end.

That deal was a masterclass in Red Zone execution. We didn't get lucky. We were prepared. That's what this chapter is about, prepping every deal to close strong.

Preparation Wins Before the Close

In football, Red Zone execution starts in the video room. Teams don't just hope to score, they plan for it. Great offenses script the right plays. They account for every scenario. Sales works the

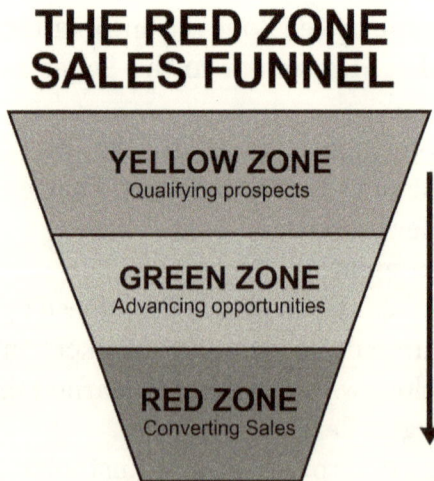

THE RED ZONE SALES FUNNEL

YELLOW ZONE
Qualifying prospects

GREEN ZONE
Advancing opportunities

RED ZONE
Converting Sales

*View your pipeline through the Zones to drive focus
and execution at every stage.*

same way. The best closers don't wait until the final call to start closing. They eliminate risk early, keep alignment tight, and ensure nothing derails the deal late.

If your deals fall apart in the final stretch, chances are it's because of a failure upstream. You missed a stakeholder. You ignored procurement. You left an objection unresolved. In the Red Zone, that's all it takes.

Play 1: Confirm Final Decision-Maker Readiness

At this point in the deal, identifying stakeholders isn't enough. You need to confirm that the people who control the outcome are fully engaged, aligned, and ready to move. That means securing the commitment of the economic buyer, understanding Procurement's role, and verifying that no surprise influencers will derail the deal late.

In early stages, it's fine to work through a champion. But in the Red Zone, champions don't close deals, economic buyers do. If that person hasn't been part of a business case review, ROI conversation, or closing call, you're exposed.

What: Before heading into the close, confirm that the final decision-maker is not just known, but involved, aligned, and ready. Ask questions like:

- *Who has the final sign-off on this agreement?*

- *Have they reviewed the proposal or seen the business case?*

- *Would it make sense to set up time with them to ensure full alignment?*

Why: You can't close a deal if the real decision-maker isn't in the game. Vague answers to these questions mean you're still guessing, and guessing in the Red Zone leads to stalled deals. Readiness means that the right people are aligned, informed, and ready to move. Otherwise, you're closing into a void.

Example: In a deal with a fast-scaling e-commerce brand, negotiations were moving, but the timeline kept slipping. I paused and asked the champion, *Who ultimately owns the decision to fund this?*

They admitted the CFO hadn't been looped in and was skeptical about the ROI. We immediately created a simple financial summary and booked a 30-minute exec briefing. That one meeting realigned the deal. The CFO requested one tweak to the payment terms, then gave the green light within a week. Had we not confirmed true decision-maker readiness, the deal would've stalled, or died.

Pro Tip: Don't assume alignment, verify it. Ask early and revisit often. If you want to score in the Red Zone, make sure the decision-makers are already standing in the end zone, ready to receive the ball.

Once you've confirmed the decision-maker is ready, the next threat comes from inside the process itself, Procurement and Legal. Getting them involved early is how you stay in control and avoid a last-minute stall.

Play 2: Engage Procurement and Legal Before It's Too Late

What: Get the Procurement and Legal groups involved before you're in final negotiations. Don't wait until the end to share terms, ask early: *What does your Procurement and Legal review process usually look like?"*

Then proactively send your standard MSA or commercial terms so they can begin redlining while the deal is still moving forward.

Why: Procurement and Legal aren't roadblocks, they're required checkpoints. But if you wait until the deal is "ready to sign," you've already lost time and control. Legal reviews can take weeks. In enterprise deals, that delay can push you into a new quarter or completely deflate urgency. Starting early keeps you in control and shortens your close cycle.

Example: One rep had executive buy-in and a verbal yes, but waited to share the agreement. Legal sat on it for two weeks, then Procurement flagged several terms, and the deal slipped into Q2, losing priority. On the next deal, the rep looped in Legal as soon as the proposal was out. With redlines addressed in parallel, they closed on time and without last-minute drama.

Pro Tip: Use this phrase as your early trigger: *We've found it helpful to start Legal and Procurement review early so that nothing holds us up at the finish line, would it make sense to share terms now?*

Even if pricing isn't final, sending your standard documents in parallel buys time and eliminates silent stall risks before they show up.

With the right people involved and the internal process in motion, the next step is creating real urgency. But instead of forcing artificial pressure, smart sellers tie the close to something that already matters to the buyer. Let's talk about how to anchor to a real business deadline.

Play 3: Anchor to a Real Business Deadline

What: Tie your close date to a business-critical milestone on the buyer's side. Think:

- A product launch
- Hiring deadline
- Compliance window
- Budget cycle
- Board meeting

Ask: *Should we work backward from a key date or milestone you're targeting?* This creates urgency that's authentic and buyer-driven.

Why: Deals don't close just because a seller *wants* them to. They close when the buyer sees value in acting *now*. If there's no real deadline, there's no urgency, and no reason to prioritize your deal. By anchoring to a buyer's internal timeline, you create natural momentum and shift from chasing to aligning.

Example: In a late-stage deal, one of our reps learned the buyer needed the platform live before a regional sales kickoff. That gave us a firm internal deadline. Instead of saying, *Can we close by the end of the month?*, we said, *To make your kickoff date, we'll need to finalize this by the 15th.* That shifted the focus from our goal to theirs. The deal closed early, because the timeline mattered to them.

Pro Tip: Use this positioning line: *To meet your [Q2 goals / launch deadline / compliance window], we'd need to finalize by [X date]. Does that timing work on your end?*

This isn't pressure, it's partnership. When your deal supports their mission-critical path, urgency becomes mutual.

Deadlines drive urgency, but urgency often brings out last-minute concerns. The best sellers don't wait for objections to pop up: They surface them early and handle them head-on. Let's look at how to take control before resistance slows you down.

Play 4: Handle Objections Proactively

What: Don't wait for objections to surface in the final hour. Proactively invite them early and often by asking targeted, disarming questions like:

- *What concerns do you have about moving forward?*
- *Who else needs to sign off, and what's their perspective?*
- *What's the biggest risk in your mind if this doesn't go well?*

This gets unspoken hesitation out in the open, while you still have time to address it.

Why: Objections rarely show up out of nowhere. They just stay unspoken until the buyer feels pressure to decide, or to walk away. Great reps surface tension early, resolve it collaboratively, and remove resistance before it becomes a deal-killer. This makes closing feel natural, not forced.

Example: One of our reps was mid-cycle with a deal that seemed strong, until the buyer went cold. In the review, we realized we never asked about internal resistance. On the next deal, the rep changed his approach and asked early: *What would cause this to stall internally?*

The buyer revealed that finance was skeptical of the ROI. That gave us a chance to build a custom cost justification and loop in the CFO. The deal closed, because we smoked out the objection early.

Pro Tip: Don't treat objections as bad news, treat them as momentum signals. The buyer is thinking deeply. They're engaging.

Try this script: *Let's play it safe for a second. From your point of view, what could derail this project?*

The earlier you ask, the more time you have to shape the narrative, earn trust, and close clean.

Once objections are addressed, it's time to make sure your buyer is still fully bought in. Momentum without commitment is just motion. Let's talk about how to lock in real alignment at every step.

Play 5: Confirm Buyer Commitment at Every Stage

What: Don't confuse interest with commitment. Just because a buyer is engaged doesn't mean they're ready to buy. Throughout the sales cycle, especially in the Red Zone, test intent by asking direct, commitment-checking questions like:

- *If we solve X and Y, is there anything that could stop us from moving forward?*

- *If we sent the contract tomorrow, would you be ready to sign?*

Why: The Red Zone is not the time to discover your buyer has doubts, blockers, or is missing approvals. If they're not ready to move forward, you need to know *now*, not at the finish line. These questions create clarity, uncover hesitation, and help you address misalignment while there's still time to course-correct.

Example: One of our reps was in the final stages of a deal and everything seemed green. But before scheduling legal review, he asked the customer: *If we sent the contract this week, would you be ready to sign?*

The buyer hesitated and admitted they still hadn't aligned with IT on deployment. That gave the rep a chance to bring IT into the loop, resolve concerns, and rebuild alignment, *before* the deal hit a wall. The close was delayed by a week, but it closed. Because he asked.

Pro Tip: Use a soft setup to avoid sounding pushy: *Before we go into final steps, can I check, if everything looks good and X is solved, is there anything that could hold this up?*

If the answer is anything but, *Nope, we're good,* dig deeper. Your job is to surface hesitation before it becomes resistance. This is how elite closers validate readiness, not just interest.

With commitment confirmed, now it's time to take full control of the finish. Great closers don't wait for deals to happen, they build the plan that makes it inevitable. Let's talk about how to own the close.

Play 6: Build and Own the Close Plan

What: Don't assume the buyer has a process. Most don't. That's your job. By the time you're in the Green

Zone, you should have created and shared a mutual action plan (MAP) with your champion. This plan should include every step, from verbal approval to engaging Procurement to go-live. Assign internal owners on their side and yours. Set hard dates. Review it weekly.

Why: Deals that stall late almost always lack structure. A solid close plan does three things:

- Creates clarity on what's next.
- Exposes friction points early.
- Drives accountability across all stakeholders.

When everyone knows the plan, and their role in it, you stay in control, even as things get complex.

Example: A rep on our team was in the Red Zone of a six-figure enterprise deal. Verbal approval was in, but nothing was moving. Instead of chasing for updates, he revisited the MAP with the champion: *Let's take 5 minutes to review our close plan, just want to make sure we're still aligned.*

That conversation surfaced two blockers: Procurement hadn't reviewed the MSA, and the executive sign-off date had shifted. Because the rep had structure, he spotted the stall early, adjusted the plan, and kept the deal alive. It closed two weeks later. No close plan? That deal would've slipped, and maybe died.

Pro Tip: Frame the MAP as a partnership tool, not a sales tactic. Say: *To make sure we don't miss anything, let's map out each step together, who's involved, what needs to happen, and when.*

Use a simple format with 4 columns:

- Step
- Owner
- Target Date
- Status

Update this weekly. If your deal doesn't have a close plan, it's not ready to close.

You've built the close plan, now the challenge is keeping it alive. Urgency fades quickly if you don't defend it. Here's how to sustain momentum and keep the pressure on through the final stretch.

Defend and Sustain Urgency Through the Final Stretch

Urgency gets a deal moving. Sustained urgency gets it across the finish line.

By the time you're in the Red Zone, you've already aligned the solution to the buyer's goals. You've shown the impact. You've helped them see why waiting costs money or market share.

But here's the reality, urgency fades fast. Priorities shift. Internal distractions pop up. What felt urgent last week suddenly gets pushed behind a new initiative. And if you don't defend that urgency, the deal stalls, right when you're about to score.

Red Zone sellers don't just create urgency, they reinforce it through the finish. That means reminding buyers why they committed to the timeline in the first place. It means re-aligning around the business case, key milestones, and opportunity cost of delay.

Here's how to keep urgency alive when it starts slipping:

- Circle back to the business impact:

   When we first connected, your goal was to launch this before your seasonal spike. Has that changed?

- Reference internal alignment:

  Your executive team was aligned on the Q2 rollout. Is there a new priority we should factor in?

- Re-anchor to buyer-driven milestones:

  If we finalize this week, your team is still on track for the April go-live. If this slips to next month, we'll likely push into June. Does that work for your internal timeline?

In one deal with a logistics software company, everything was set. Procurement was engaged, legal was moving, and we had verbal sign-off from the COO. Then silence. Two weeks with no movement. When I reconnected, I found out another internal project had jumped the line.

I didn't push. I walked back through their own business case, the revenue targets they needed to hit, the operational gap we were solving, the training runway they required. We re-established the timeline, and the contract was signed four days later.

Urgency isn't a one-time tactic. In the Red Zone, it's something you defend. You reinforce. You re-energize.

When urgency stays alive, deals stay in motion. And motion is what closes.

Play 7: Reinforce Confidence in the Decision

What: As you approach the close, buyers can get nervous. That's normal. They start thinking about risk, post-purchase regret, and internal scrutiny. Your job isn't to push harder, it's to reassure smarter. Reinforce their decision by reminding them of the value and showing what happens after signature.

Tactics that work:

- Resurface the business case and ROI you built earlier.

- Share relevant case studies or testimonials.

- Offer a quick intro to a happy customer.

- Walk them through onboarding and support in detail.

Why: A confident buyer is a committed buyer. When they feel secure in the decision, a buyer will move faster and with fewer delays. If they're unsure, even subconsciously, they'll stall, loop in new voices, or start second-guessing. Your role is to remove the unknowns, rebuild belief, and lead them through the finish.

Example: One of our reps had a deal nearly derailed in the final week. The buyer had verbal sign-off, but then the Legal group started asking questions that felt like stall tactics. Instead of pushing, the rep said: *Before we finalize, would it be helpful to see what onboarding looks like from day one?*

The rep walked the buyer through the timeline, deliverables, and team involved. They then shared a two-minute customer video where a similar company talked about their success in the first 90 days. The buyer relaxed, refocused, and signed a week later. Why? Because they felt confident and supported.

Pro Tip: Use this check-in line: *On a scale of 1–10, how confident are you in moving forward right now?*

If it's anything less than a 9, follow up with: *What would make it a 10?* Then deliver the reassurance they need, proof, clarity, and a path forward. Don't push, reinforce.

Red Zone readiness isn't just about preparation, it's about control. You've now got the plays to align decision-makers, eliminate friction, and create urgency before it's too late. Let's recap the moves that make closing feel like a formality, not a fight.

Chapter Recap

- Red Zone readiness means preparing your deal to close, long before you're actually closing.

- Identify every decision-maker and gain access early. Don't rely on a single champion.

- Loop in Legal and Procurement before they become roadblocks.

- Anchor to real business deadlines to create urgency that moves the deal forward.

- Handle objections proactively, not reactively.

- When internal chaos slows the deal down, bring the process. Lead your buyer through the finish.

Red Zone Drills:

Drill 1: Build a Close Plan

Choose one active deal that's in the final stretch. Build a mutual action plan with your champion. Include each step to close, target dates, and responsible parties. Review it together and update it weekly.

Drill 2: Surface Objections

For one active opportunity, ask your prospect directly: "Before we move to contract, is there anything that could slow us down or get flagged internally?" Flush it out now, before it becomes a surprise.

Drill 3: Anchor to a Milestone

Review your pipeline and identify one deal where the timeline is vague. Create urgency by tying the close to a buyer-driven business event. Update your messaging accordingly.

Drill 4: Confidence Boost

Identify a deal where the buyer is hesitating. Offer a customer reference call, share a relevant case study, or walk them through a transition plan. Reinforce that moving forward is a smart, low-risk decision.

Preparation creates confidence. Confidence creates execution. Execution wins deals.

No matter how well you've prepared, there comes a point in every deal when the clock is winding down. Pressure mounts. The buyer hesitates. Internal priorities shift. Legal redlines pile up. This is where deals are won or lost, not because of the product, but because of how you perform when time is short and the stakes are high.

This is the Two-Minute Drill. It's your final drive, the moment where urgency, precision, and control matter most. The deals that close in the final stretch aren't closed by luck. They're closed by sales pros who stay calm under pressure, guide the process with clarity, and execute like champions.

In the next chapter, we'll break down how to run the Two-Minute Drill, how to keep control when the buyer is wobbling, how to eliminate distractions, and how to move from verbal yes to signed contract without dropping the ball.

Let's finish the drive.

Get access to the Red Zone Selling Resource Center including templates, scripts, and playbooks at redzoneselling.co.

CHAPTER 8

The Two-Minute Drill

Execute Under Pressure

If we're talking about the greatest at executing under pressure, the conversation has to include Tom Brady.

As a New York Giants fan, I can say we were fortunate in our Super Bowl wins against New England to have kept the ball out of Brady's hands in the final minutes. If he had the ball for two minutes or more, the outcome might have been different. Just ask the Atlanta Falcons.

In Super Bowl LI (2017), the Falcons held what seemed like an insurmountable 28-3 lead with 8:31 left in the third quarter. But Brady and the Patriots didn't panic. They chipped away at the lead, scoring 25 unanswered points to force overtime. On the final drive of regulation, Brady got the ball back with just two minutes left. Starting from his own 25-yard line, he orchestrated a flawless drive, completing key passes, managing the clock, and ultimately setting up a game-tying touchdown with 58 seconds left. The Patriots won in overtime, completing the greatest comeback in Super Bowl history.

Brady's performance wasn't about luck. It was about execution. He understood the urgency of the moment but didn't rush. He knew how to control the game, make decisive plays, and systematically break down the defense, even with the clock winding down.

This is exactly what top sales professionals do when a deal is in the final moments. They know that when time is running out, there's no room for hesitation, confusion, or unnecessary delays. This is the Two-Minute Drill where deals are won or lost.

In football, the two-minute drill isn't just about speed; it's about precision, confidence, and control. The quarterback must:

- Read the defense quickly: Identify weak spots and exploit them.
- Make fast, decisive plays: There's no time for second-guessing.
- Control the tempo: Keep the defense on its heels and maintain momentum.
- Execute flawlessly under pressure: Every move must be deliberate and effective.

In sales, closing a deal in the final stretch works the same way. You need to recognize when the clock is running out whether it's the end of the quarter, a competitor making a last-minute move, or a shift in your prospect's priorities. The best sellers don't panic; they take control of the conversation, remove roadblocks, and guide the buyer to a clear and confident decision.

Many deals stall in the final minutes because sales reps hesitate, introduce unnecessary steps, or fail to create a sense of urgency. Your ability to execute in crunch time is what separates elite closers from those who let deals slip away.

The key to mastering the Two-Minute Drill is understanding how to drive decisions quickly, making sure your prospect feels ready and confident to move forward before doubt, distractions, or delays creep in.

In the next section, we'll break down how to drive decisions quickly, so when the game is on the line and the pressure is at its highest, you can lead your prospect into the end zone and close the deal with confidence.

As Billie Jean King said, *Pressure is a privilege.*[4] She should know, she won more than 20 championships!

Play 1: Master the Clock

What: In the final stretch, time becomes your most valuable resource. Elite sellers don't wait, they work the timeline like a weapon. You must know how much time you have, what steps remain, and how to compress the close without cutting corners.

Why: Deals die in the final moments when timelines slip. If you don't control the clock, someone, or something, else will. Elite closers compress the close by anchoring to a buyer-driven deadline and working backward to eliminate surprises.

Example: Anchor to the buyer's go-live date, then ask:

- How long does the legal review typically take?

- When does Procurement need to be involved?

- Are there any calendar gaps coming up (such as executive travel, end-of-quarter freeze, or holidays)?

Set micro-deadlines: *If we want this signed by Friday, we need redlines by Wednesday and verbal approval by Thursday.*

Embed these steps in your Mutual Action Plan (MAP) and reconfirm them often.

---

[4] *Pressure is a Privilege: Lessons I've Learned from Life and the Battle of the Sexes*, Billie Jean King and Christine Brennan (2008).

Pro Tip: Control the clock without becoming a pest. Check in early and often:

"Just checking, are we still on track for redlines by Wednesday?"

Pacing beats chasing.

When you master the clock, you create urgency. But urgency alone isn't enough, you need to remove every ounce of friction. That's where the No-Huddle Close comes in.

Play 2: Run a No-Huddle Close

What: The No-Huddle Close is about eliminating delays and speeding up every step of the closing process. Like a football team running plays without a huddle, you keep the tempo high and the defense (your competition) off-balance.

Why: Deals often die because sellers wait for buyers to "circle back" or "run it by the team." In the Red Zone, you can't afford dead air. Speed wins. Simplify the process, remove bottlenecks, and keep the deal moving forward without pause.

Example: Pre-build a Closing Checklist: Confirm pricing, decision-makers, and prep the contract in advance.

- **Get all stakeholders in the room (or on Zoom):** Legal, Procurement, and executives, no gaps, no waiting.

- **Accelerate Communication:** Use same-day follow-ups, texts, WhatsApp, or Slack instead of slow email threads.

Act like time is running out, because it is.

Pro Tip: Before your final meetings, send an agenda that highlights: *Our goal today is to align final details and move directly to sign-off.* This sets the expectation that today's meeting isn't exploratory, it's decisive.

I remember a deal I was working on with a fast-growing SaaS company in the productivity space. We were in the final stages, verbal approval from the champion, pricing agreed, contract in Procurement's hands. We were just days away from getting the signature.

Then I noticed something subtle: The tone of my champion's emails changed. Replies took longer. The energy we had built throughout the deal started to fade. Everything looked right on the surface, but something felt off.

Instead of assuming we were still on track, I sent a simple message: *Are we still aligned to move forward by the end of the week? Just want to make sure we're still heading toward that timeline.*

He replied: *We're still very interested, but our CFO flagged some concerns about timing, given a few internal initiatives that just came up.* Ugh. A gut punch but not insurmountable.

If I hadn't asked, I would've walked into the end of the week expecting a contract, and come away empty-handed. That message gave me the opening to re-engage at the executive level. We scheduled a quick meeting with the CFO, walked them through the projected ROI, and reframed the conversation around short-term gains and implementation simplicity.

We agreed on a revised implementation date, got the go ahead, and signed the deal a week later.

The lesson? Buyer intent is never static. Priorities shift. Internal dynamics change. If you don't stop to reconfirm commitment mid-drive, you risk running a perfect play, only to find out the goalposts moved.

If priorities have shifted or internal pushback has emerged, you need to know now, not after the quarter closes. Redirect the conversation. Revalidate the timeline. Keep your finger on the pulse.

Sometimes, even with a fast tempo, the defense stiffens. When deals start dragging or buyers get overwhelmed, it's not time to push harder, it's time to call a strategic timeout.

Play 3: Call the Timeout

What: When momentum slows, great closers don't push harder, they pause strategically. Calling a timeout means taking a step back to realign, reset expectations, and remove confusion before it derails the deal.

Why: When buyers get overwhelmed, decisions stall, Legal bogs down, and stakeholders disengage. A well-timed timeout isn't passive, it's proactive. It allows you to clarify priorities, reinforce urgency, and get everyone back on the same page.

Example: Use a timeout to ask:

- *Let's pause for 15 minutes to realign on what success looks like.*

- *Can we do a quick touchpoint with your CFO to confirm we're aligned?*

- *What's really holding this up?*

- *Let's review how we got here and your goals.*

These resets often unlock the path forward when deals get stuck.

Pro Tip: Plan your timeout just like you plan your closing moves. Never wing it. Go in with one goal:

Reset clarity → Rebuild urgency → Accelerate decision.

Timeouts aren't about slowing down, they're about speeding up the right way.

You've built urgency, managed the clock, and kept momentum. Now it's time to tighten the game plan even further, and eliminate anything that could cost you the win.

Play 4: Eliminate the Extra Play

What: When the clock is ticking, you don't add plays, you simplify. Late-stage selling is about compression, not expansion. Cut anything that doesn't drive the deal straight to signature.

Why: Extra meetings, pilot extensions, or looping in new stakeholders can feel productive, but they often mask hesitation. Every unnecessary step slows momentum, creates new risks, and opens the door for the deal to stall or slip away.

Example: Before agreeing to any new step, ask yourself:

- *Will this step bring us closer to signature, or further away?*
- *Is this new stakeholder necessary, or a distraction?*
- *Does this request indicate interest, or avoidance?*

If it doesn't shorten the path to closed-won, it doesn't belong.

Pro Tip: In the Red Zone, be ruthless with your cycle. Politely but firmly push back on unnecessary steps:

Let's stay focused on the original path we agreed on to meet your timeline.

Cut the fluff. Compress the cycle. Finish the drive.

You're inside the Red Zone now. The margin for error is gone. Mastering the clock, eliminating friction, and staying ruthlessly focused are what separate closers from almost-closers. Let's recap the key plays you need to finish the drive.

Chapter Recap

- Time is your enemy in the final stretch. Control it.
- Run a no-huddle offense. Remove friction and simplify steps.
- Reconfirm commitment before pushing to the close.
- Use a Two-Minute Summary to reinforce value and create clarity.
- Call a timeout when confusion or delays arise.
- Eliminate any extra steps that don't directly move the deal forward.

Red Zone Drills:

Drill 1: Timeline Compression

Take one active deal. Create a reverse timeline working backwards from kickoff back to getting the contract. Identify micro-deadlines and pressure points that could slow down the close.

TIMELINE COMPRESSION	
Create a reverse timeline from implementation to contract. Identify micro-deadlines and pressure points that could slow down the close	
IMPLEMENTATION DATE	October 5
CONTRACT SIGNED	September 21
CONTRACT REVIEW	September 14
VERBAL	September 5
WHERE YOU ARE	TODAY

Use timeline compression to create urgency, shorten the sales cycle, and close deals faster.

Drill 2: Friction Audit

List every open step in your nearest-to-close deal. Highlight any step that adds time but not value. Cut it or streamline it.

Drill 3: Commitment Checkpoint

Send a message to your champion asking: "Are we still aligned to move forward by [target date]?" Use their response to guide your next move.

When the clock is winding down and your prospect is on the edge of a decision, it's not about being perfect, it's about being prepared. The Two-Minute Drill separates closers from chokers.

And if all else fails, if the clock hits zero and you're still not in the end zone, there's one last move in your arsenal.

In the next chapter, we'll cover *The Hail Mary*, when to take a bold, calculated shot to salvage a deal before it slips away.

Get access to the Red Zone Selling Resource Center including templates, scripts, and playbooks at redzoneselling.co.

CHAPTER 9

The Hail Mary

When and How to Go Bold

The term "Hail Mary" carries weight in both faith and football.

In Catholic tradition, the Hail Mary is a prayer for divine intervention, often recited in moments of need. In football, it's the ultimate desperation play, a long, high-risk pass thrown into the end zone with little time left on the clock, hoping for a miracle

Few quarterbacks have mastered the Hail Mary like Aaron Rodgers. As of the 2024 season, he has thrown four successful Hail Mary touchdowns, more than any other player in NFL history. One of his most memorable came in an October 2024 game against the Detroit Lions. With time expiring, Rodgers launched a towering pass into the end zone, threading it through defenders to secure a shocking last-second victory. It was the kind of play that leaves fans in awe and opponents devastated.

But just like in football, the Hail Mary in sales should only be used when absolutely necessary. It's not a first option or a go-to strategy. It's a calculated risk, reserved for when time is running out and more conventional plays have failed. The key is knowing when to pull the trigger.

Some deals drag past deadlines, buyers go dark, or key decision-makers suddenly push back after months of progress. In those moments, standard follow-ups and logical appeals may not be enough. That's when you need a bold, all-or-nothing move to revive the opportunity and give yourself a shot at winning.

But how do you know when it's time to go for it? In the next section, we'll break that down.

Hockey great Wayne Gretzky said: *You miss 100% of the shots you don't take.*[5] Gretzky should know, as he was one of the greatest goal scorers in the history of the NHL.

Recognizing When a High-Risk Move is the Best Play

In football, coaches don't call a Hail Mary on the first drive of the game. It's a last-resort play, used when there's no other choice but to take a big swing. The same applies in sales. High-risk moves are not for everyday negotiations. They're for moments when a deal is slipping away, and conventional tactics aren't working. The key is recognizing when the situation calls for bold action instead of safe, incremental plays.

Not every stalled deal requires a drastic measure, but there are clear signs when it might be time to take a big risk:

- The buyer has gone completely silent after months of engagement, and traditional follow-ups aren't working.

- A competitor has gained an edge, and you need to shake things up to stay in the game.

- A key decision-maker has changed, bringing uncertainty to the deal.

- The prospect is hesitant, stuck in indecision, or afraid to make the final commitment.

- Budget constraints have surfaced, threatening to kill the opportunity.

---

[5] Gretzky, Wayne. As quoted in various interviews and featured in *The Great One: The Complete Wayne Gretzky Collection*, Triumph Books, 2000.

HAIL MARY CHECKLIST
Sign when it might be time to take a big risk.
✓ Buyer has gone completely silent
✓ Competitor has edged ahead
✓ Key decision-maker has changed
✓ Prospect is stuck in indecision
✓ Budget constraints have surfaced
Touchdown!

Use the Hail Mary Checklist as a last-resort play
to revive stalled deals and take a bold shot at closing.

Recognizing these moments isn't just about desperation: It's about timing. A well-placed high-risk move can reignite momentum, push a buyer to act, or even turn a lost deal into a closed one. So, what does a Hail Mary in sales look like?

- It could be an all-in pricing adjustment that creates a now-or-never moment.
- It might be a direct appeal to the CEO when lower-level contacts have stalled.
- It could be a bold, unexpected value-add that forces reconsideration.
- It could be a promise to build an anticipated feature on the road map.

The key is that it's a big move, not just another nudge.

Taking a high-risk shot doesn't guarantee a win, but when time is running out, it may be the only play left. Next, we'll dive into how to create an offer so irresistible that you win the deal.

NOTE: I'm intentionally breaking from the standard "Play" format here to give you a deeper, more detailed breakdown. Executing the perfect Hail Mary requires a different level of precision, and this section gives you everything you need to pull it off.

Play 1: Crafting an Irresistible Offer to Win the Deal

When a game is on the line, great quarterbacks don't just throw the ball. They put it where only their receiver can catch it. In sales, when a deal is slipping away, you need to craft an offer so compelling that the buyer feels they'd be making a mistake by saying no. This is the ultimate power move, a strategic, high-impact play that forces a decision in your favor.

An irresistible offer isn't just about discounts or last-minute incentives. It's about framing value in a way that speaks directly to what the buyer needs at that moment. The goal is to eliminate hesitation, neutralize objections, and create a scenario where moving forward is the obvious choice.

There are different ways to execute this:

- **Risk Reversal:** Reduce the buyer's fear by offering a money-back guarantee, a trial period, or a phased roll-out. This shifts the risk from them to you, making the decision easier.

- **Exclusive Access:** Provide something unique they can't get anywhere else, such as priority onboarding, VIP support, a Client Advisory Board (CAB) position, or a feature to which they wouldn't normally have access.

- **Urgency Play:** Use real, legitimate scarcity, whether this is limited availability, pricing that expires, or implementation slots that will fill up. The key is that what's scarce must be real, not a gimmick.

- **Personalized Concessions:** Instead of a generic discount, tailor the offer to their specific concerns. Maybe its extended payment terms, additional training, or bundling in extra services.

One offer that has worked for me over the years is the "competitive buy-out play." Use this strategy when a buyer is still under contract with a core competitor, typically for six months to a year, and cannot exit early. In this scenario, the buyer recognizes your solution is better, but is contractually bound to an existing alternative.

To overcome this, offer a buyout of their existing contract. Instead of absorbing the cost upfront, extend their new agreement to offset the buyout amount. For example, if the buyout is $100,000 and your standard offer is $200,000 over two years, extend the term to three years to recover the cost. This approach mitigates the buyout expense while securing a long-term commitment.

The best power moves aren't just about giving something away. They're about making the buyer feel like they're winning. If you've done your job right, your offer should feel like a no-brainer.

But not every bold play works. Sometimes, even the best-crafted offer doesn't land. In those moments, the real test is how you recover.

Play 2: When to Take the Shot to the Top

Sometimes, the most powerful Hail Mary isn't a discount or incentive, it's a direct line to power.

When a deal is stuck in the weeds, decision-makers go dark, or internal politics start to stall momentum, one of the boldest and most effective moves you can make is taking your message straight to the top.

But this play is high-risk, high-reward. You don't escalate casually. You escalate with precision, purpose, and a clear value-driven message.

I've used this move a handful of times in my career, and each time it was a calculated decision, not an act of desperation. One memorable instance was with a large fintech company. We had strong traction with the operations and IT teams, and our champion was fully bought in. But for weeks, the deal sat in Procurement limbo. Calls slowed. Emails became vague. It became clear that internal priorities were shifting and we were losing momentum.

I decided to go for it.

With guidance from my champion, I reached out directly to the COO. I sent a short, focused email outlining the business impact of our solution, the risk of delay, and the strategic advantage they'd lose by pushing this into the next quarter. I framed it not as a sales pitch, but as a partner looking out for their business goals. I also made sure to let him know how professional his team was, and how they were looking out for the best interest of the company.

To my surprise, the COO responded within hours. He appreciated the directness, looped in Procurement leadership, and within three days, the deal was signed.

The lesson? Sometimes, the only way to break the deadlock is to bypass it entirely.

Here's when to take the shot to the top:

- You've already earned strong internal support, but execution is stalling.
- You've uncovered misalignment between departments or internal blockers.

- The opportunity is strategically important to the buyer's business, and you can tie your outreach to that vision.
- The buyer's executive team has shown public interest in solving the problem you're addressing.

Now, here's how to do it right:

- **Keep your message short, clear, and high-level.** Focus on business outcomes, not product features.
- **Show respect for the process.** Acknowledge the work their team has done. Be clear that you're escalating this only because the timeline or value is at risk.
- **Include a compelling reason for urgency.** This could be an upcoming market event, a risk exposure, or an opportunity window.
- **Offer a next step, not a demand.** *Happy to reconnect with your team to finalize* is more effective than *we need to close this now.*

And here's what *not* to do:

- **Don't blindside your champion.** Wherever possible, let them know you're escalating, or even better, get their support.
- **Don't escalate too early.** If you haven't done the work at lower levels, an executive will see right through the move.
- **Don't lead with discounts.** Executives care about impact and risk, not pricing tweaks.

A precision escalation can be the difference between a stalled opportunity and a closed deal. But like a Hail Mary, it requires timing, confidence, and preparation. You have to read the field, pick your spot, and throw a perfect pass.

It's not a play you use often, but when you do, make it count.

Play 3: How to Recover and Pivot When Bold Plays Don't Land

Not every bold move results in a game-winning touchdown. In football, when a Hail Mary falls incomplete, the team doesn't quit; they regroup, analyze what went wrong, and adjust for the next opportunity. The same applies in sales. Throwing a key pass and missing your receiver doesn't mean failure; it means learning, refining your strategy, and staying in the game.

High-risk moves are, by nature, unpredictable. Sometimes they spark urgency and flip a deal in your favor. Other times, they don't land as expected. A prospect may reject your offer, double down on indecision, or even go with a competitor despite your best efforts. How you respond in these moments is what separates top performers from average sellers.

When a bold play doesn't work, resist the urge to go silent. Instead, step back and assess why:

- Did the prospect reject the offer outright, or was there hesitation?
- Was the timing wrong? Or, was the move itself off the mark?
- Did external factors, budget changes, leadership shifts, or internal politics play a bigger role than expected?
- What did you learn about the buyer's real priorities and objections?

Once you've analyzed the outcome, the next step is to pivot. That could mean re-engaging with a new angle, shifting focus to a different decision-maker, or shelving the deal temporarily while maintaining the relationship.

Great sales professionals don't let a lost deal define them. They use setbacks as fuel, sharpening their instincts for the next opportunity. Every bold attempt provides valuable insights, whether it results in a win or a lesson.

Chapter Recap

- A Hail Mary in sales is not a first option; it's a calculated risk used when a deal is slipping away.

- Situations that may call for a Hail Mary include unresponsive buyers, competitive threats, last-minute decision-maker changes, or budget constraints.

- Effective Hail Mary plays in sales include all-in pricing adjustments, direct CEO engagement, bold value-adds, and competitive buy-outs.

- The ultimate power move is crafting an irresistible offer that eliminates hesitation and forces a decision in your favor.

- If a Hail Mary doesn't land, top sales professionals analyze, adapt, and pivot rather than giving up.

Red Zone Drills:

Drill 1: Designing Your Hail Mary Offer

List potential high-impact moves for a deal at risk (e.g., risk-reversal guarantees, VIP access, competitive buy-out).

Ensure the offer is time-sensitive and compelling enough to push for immediate action.

Drill 2: Put Your Offer Into Action

Craft a direct, no-fluff message to your prospect outlining the bold move you're willing to make.

The Hail Mary is about calculated risk, not desperation. When executed correctly, it can turn a near-lost deal into a major win. But even if it doesn't work, great closers use every attempt as a learning experience, refining their instincts for the next big opportunity. It's your turn. When the deal is on the line, will you take the shot?

But here's the thing, pulling off a game-changing play in the final moments isn't just about having the right strategy. It's about having the right mentality. The greatest closers don't just react to high-pressure situations, they thrive in them. They don't flinch. They don't second-guess. They step up with total confidence, knowing they've put in the work and trust their ability to execute.

That's what separates the elite from the average. And that's what we're diving into next, the Closer Mentality. If you want to win consistently, you need to think, act, and operate like a closer every single day. Let's break that down.

Get access to the Red Zone Selling Resource Center including templates, scripts, and playbooks at redzoneselling.co.

CHAPTER 10

Closer Mentality

Enter the Sandman

No one in the history of Major League Baseball (MLB) was as fierce a closer as Mariano Rivera of the New York Yankees. Rivera holds the MLB record for most career saves at 652, and he also boasts a career save percentage of 89%. That means he was *lights out* nearly 9 out of 10 times when he took the mound!

Now, you might be wondering why we're stepping off the football field and onto the baseball diamond here. Simple: If we're talking about a closer's mentality, there's no better example than Mariano Rivera. When the pressure was at its absolute highest, Rivera was the gold standard for execution, focus, and finishing the job.

Imagine you're a big-league hitter, standing in the on-deck circle. You hear Metallica's *Enter the Sandman* blaring over the loudspeakers, the crowd roaring, as Rivera jogs in from the bullpen. You step into the batter's box knowing you're about to face the filthiest cutter in baseball history. Rivera's presence alone was intimidating. His execution was lethal.

Now, imagine bringing that same level of composure, precision, and inevitability to sales. That's what it takes to be an elite closer.

Great closers don't just rely on skill, they master their *mindset*. When the pressure is high and the game is on the line, they don't flinch. In sales, the final stages of a deal in the Red Zone are where champions are made. Here's what separates elite closers from the rest:

Short-Term Memory & Resilience

Rivera once said: *You have to forget about the last pitch. The next one is the most important.*[6] Sales is no different. Deals won't always go your way. Prospects will ghost you, objections will arise, and competitors will undercut you at the last minute. Average reps dwell on lost deals, but elite closers reset, refocus, and move on.

Confidence Without Arrogance

Rivera threw essentially *one* pitch his entire career, but he mastered it to the point where hitters *knew* what was coming and still couldn't hit it. That's confidence. In sales, confidence comes from mastering your process, knowing your buyer, anticipating objections, and delivering value with conviction. The best closers don't just *think* they'll win; they *know* they've done the work to deserve it.

Calm Under Pressure

The ninth inning in baseball is like the Red Zone in sales, it's where deals are won or lost. Pressure mounts, stakes rise, and nerves kick in. Lesser sales reps panic when a deal stalls or a last-minute objection surfaces. Elite closers stay calm, stick to their process, and guide the prospect across the finish line.

---

[6] Rivera, Mariano. *The Closer: My Story*. Little, Brown and Company, 2014.

Like Rivera perfected his cutter, you can train your mind to thrive under pressure:

- **Visualize the Win**, Top athletes mentally rehearse success before stepping onto the field. Before a big sales call, *see* yourself handling objections, driving urgency, and closing with confidence.

- **Control the Controllables**, You can't stop a competitor from dropping their price at the last second, but you *can* control how you respond. Stay focused on what you can influence.

- **Trust the Process**, Rivera didn't try to reinvent his pitch in the ninth inning, he trusted what worked. Stick to your sales playbook, execute with precision, and don't second-guess yourself when it's time to close.

Become the Mariano Rivera of Sales

As Paul "Bear" Bryant the legendary football coach from Alabama is famous for saying: *Everybody has the will to win, but not everybody has the will to prepare to win.*[7]

Mariano Rivera didn't just win, he *expected* to win. That's the mindset of a true closer. Develop the discipline, master your approach, and when it's your time to seal the deal, step up with confidence.

Mariano Rivera never waited for the game to come to him, he took control. The best closers don't sit back and react; they dictate the pace, set the tone, and impose their will. That's the difference between playing offense and playing defense in sales.

Too many sales reps operate defensively, waiting for the prospect to make a move. They hesitate to push for next steps,

---

[7] Bryant, Paul "Bear". Widely attributed. Commonly cited in sports leadership literature as a reflection of his emphasis on preparation over desire.

hoping the buyer will take the initiative. This reactive mindset leads to stalled deals, ghosting, and lost momentum.

Elite closers? They *play to win*. They take ownership of the deal and drive it forward with intention.

Playing defense in sales looks like this:

- Waiting for the prospect to follow up after a demo.
- Asking, *Let me know if you have any questions,* instead of guiding the next steps.
- Accepting *Let me think about it* without addressing the hesitation head-on.
- Allowing Procurement or Legal to dictate the timeline, instead of setting clear expectations.

Defensive sellers let the buyer control the deal, which almost always leads to delays, indecision, and ultimately, lost opportunities.

Great closers, on the other hand, *run the offense.* They dictate the tempo and lead the buyer toward a decision with confidence.

Play 1: Play to Win, Not to Avoid Losing

What: Elite closers play to win. Average reps play not to lose. There's a massive difference. Playing to win means driving the conversation, taking control of the close, and pushing confidently for decisions. Playing not to lose means hesitating, deferring, and hoping things work out.

Why: When you're trying to avoid a loss:

- You play it safe.
- You defer hard conversations.
- You over-accommodate buyer requests.
- You hope Legal doesn't derail things.

- You delay asking for the close because you're afraid of hearing "no."

This defensive posture leads to stalls, ghosting, and deals that die slow, painful deaths. Top performers don't sit back and wait for good things to happen, *they make them happen.* They accept that hearing "no," is a possibility, but they push hard for a clear outcome.

Example: In one enterprise deal I worked, we were neck-and-neck with a competitor. Our champion started hesitating, asking for more time, and revisiting old objections. Instead of backing off, I leaned in and said:

Can I be honest? It sounds like you're trying to protect against making the wrong decision. But the real risk is standing still. If we're not the right fit, I'll respect that. But if we are, let's win this together.

That direct conversation shifted the energy. He re-engaged his team and we closed two weeks later.

Pro Tip: Confidence creates momentum. Don't tiptoe around the close. Step into it. Buyers take their emotional cues from you. If you act tentative, they'll hesitate. If you act decisive, they'll follow.

Playing to win starts with your mindset. But winning consistently requires a game plan built around offense, not defense. Let's talk about how to play offense in sales, and take control of the deal from start to finish.

Play 2: How to Play Offense in Sales

What: Playing offense in sales means you don't wait for the buyer to dictate the process, you proactively lead it. Offensive-minded reps shape the buying journey, control the clock, and eliminate friction before it appears.

Why: When you react to the buyer's moves, you lose control. Deals stall, priorities shift, and competitors slip in. Elite closers move first, set the agenda, surface objections early, and anchor urgency to outcomes. They drive the deal forward instead of defending against setbacks.

Example: Set the Agenda and Lead the Conversation:

Top salespeople don't just show up to calls, they own them.

Instead of asking: *What would you like to discuss today?*, they lead with: *Here's what we're going to cover, and by the end of this call, we'll align on next steps.*

This subtle shift puts you in command, and the buyer follows your game plan.

Anticipate and Address Objections Early:

Stay three steps ahead. Don't wait for objections, surface them proactively:

Instead of waiting for procurement to bog you down, say:

In my experience, legal reviews can cause delays. How can we get that process started now so it doesn't slow us down later?

Instead of waiting for pricing concerns to explode late, say:

Many clients ask about ROI at this stage. Let's walk through how we deliver measurable value right now.

By addressing friction early, you keep momentum on your side.

Control the Clock and Create Urgency:

Elite closers don't ask for the close, they show why waiting hurts.

Instead of timidly saying: *Would you like to move forward this month?*, they frame the discussion like this:

If we start this month, you'll be fully ramped by Q2 and positioned for success. Waiting means losing another quarter of potential revenue. Let's lock in the timeline to maximize impact.

Urgency tied to outcomes shifts the buyer's thinking from *Should I buy?* to *Can I afford to wait?*

Pro Tip: Every time you engage a buyer, ask yourself: *Am I driving this deal forward, or reacting to it?*

If you're reacting, you're on defense. Offensive selling wins the close.

You've built the right mindset. You've learned how to play offense. Now it's time to step up and finish the job. When the game is on the line, real closers don't hesitate, they take control and own the close.

Play 3: Own the Close

What: When the pressure peaks, true closers step up and control the moment. They don't wait for deals to close themselves, they guide, lead, and execute with confidence. In sales, you can either control the deal or let the deal control you. Own the close.

Why: The final stages of a deal are filled with pressure:

- Decision-makers hesitate.
- Competitors swoop in.

- Legal throws last-minute roadblocks.

Average reps crack. Elite closers thrive. The difference isn't who feels pressure, it's who performs under it.

Example: Picture the ninth inning. One-run lead. Two outs. The crowd is deafening.

Mariano Rivera steps onto the mound knowing that one mistake could cost his team everything. Lesser pitchers might crack, but not Rivera. He didn't just handle pressure, he turned it into fuel.

In sales, you must do the same.

When the pressure hits:

- **Don't overthink.** Stay committed to your game plan.
- **Don't panic or start discounting.** Protect your value.
- **Don't get defensive.** Stay composed and confident.
- **Don't rush the close.** Guide the buyer decisively across the finish line.

Pro Tip: Pressure doesn't create champions, it reveals them.

You won't eliminate pressure; you must learn to channel it.

Every critical deal moment is an opportunity to prove you're the closer you trained to be.

Pressure is part of every big moment. The question isn't whether you'll feel it, it's how you'll respond. Let's break down how elite closers turn pressure into their ultimate weapon.

Play 4: Turn Pressure into Your Closing Advantage

What: Pressure is inevitable in sales. Elite closers don't fear it, they embrace it, control it, and use it to win. They reframe pressure as an opportunity to showcase their preparation, stick to their process, and create urgency tied to buyer success, not panic or desperation.

Why: When stakes are high, average reps panic and rush. Elite closers slow down, stay calm, and elevate their performance. They don't let pressure make them defensive, they stay on offense, guiding the buyer confidently across the finish line.

Example:

- **Reframe Pressure as Opportunity:**

  Pressure isn't your enemy. It's your stage.

  Next time nerves kick in before a big call, tell yourself:

  This is my moment. I've trained for this. I control the outcome.

- **Stick to Your Process, Don't Panic:**

  Just like Mariano Rivera trusted his cutter under pressure, you must trust your closing framework.

  ○ Keep your tone calm and controlled.

  ○ Focus on the buyer's success, not just your commission.

  ○ Don't scramble or abandon your structure, the buyer senses everything.

- **Slow Down to Speed Up:**

  Under pressure, don't rush.

When faced with last-minute stalls, slow the pace and ask thoughtful questions like:

I completely understand this is an important decision. What's the cost of doing nothing?

Give the buyer space to process. Pressure them to think, not to panic.

- **Create Urgency Without Creating Anxiety:**

  Always tie urgency to outcomes, not desperation.

  Instead of saying: *We really need to close by Friday,* say: *Locking this in by Friday ensures your team is set up for success next quarter.*

  This frames the timeline as a benefit to them, not a need for you.

Pro Tip: Pressure reveals your preparation.

Role-play high-stakes scenarios, master your mindset, and drill your process until it's automatic.

When the game is on the line, buyers don't just hear your words, they feel your confidence.

Train Yourself to Think Like a Closer

Being a closer isn't about personality, it's about discipline. Elite closers train their minds to lead with clarity, act with confidence, and finish deals with intention. They don't wait to be told it's time to close, they drive the process from the start.

Many reps enter the Red Zone hoping things will go their way. They're passive, polite, and vague. Closers? They're direct, decisive, and focused. They don't wonder if a deal will close, they work to make sure it does.

If you want to think like a closer, develop these habits:

- **End every meeting with clear next steps**.

  Never leave a call without confirming the next action:

  Let's get a 30-minute follow-up on the calendar for next Tuesday, does that work?

- **Set deadlines to create focus.**

  Anchor discussions to business-driven milestones:

  To be live by Q2, we need to get Procurement's final signoff by [date].

- **Push with purpose**.

  Confidence isn't pressure, it's leadership: *Let's align on a decision by Friday so we stay ahead of [priority]. Sound good?*

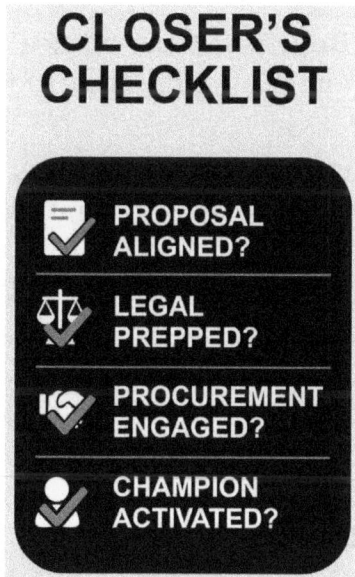

CLOSER'S CHECKLIST

- PROPOSAL ALIGNED?
- LEGAL PREPPED?
- PROCUREMENT ENGAGED?
- CHAMPION ACTIVATED?

The Closer's Checklist ensures every box is checked before you make your final move to win the deal.

Great closers don't wing it. They run their process, guide the buyer, and stay calm under pressure. It's not about being aggressive, it's about being in control.

You don't drift into closing. You commit to it. Then you train until it becomes second nature.

Closing under pressure isn't about luck, it's about preparation, mindset, and execution. You either rise to the moment or you let it slip away. Let's recap the keys to thinking and executing like a true closer.

Chapter Recap

- **Master Pressure:** Pressure doesn't break elite closers, it sharpens them. Stay calm, composed, and in control when it matters most.

- **Play to Win:** Don't play defense. Drive the process, push for clear outcomes, and close with confidence.

- **Lead the Buyer:** Set the agenda, anticipate objections early, and control the clock to keep deals moving forward.

- **Trust Your Process:** Stick to your game plan under pressure. Discipline and preparation beat panic every time.

- **Think Like a Closer:** End every call with next steps, anchor urgency to outcomes, and lead with conviction, not hope.

Red Zone Drills

Drill 1: Confidence Calibration

Record yourself pitching your solution. Watch the video and critique how confident you sound. Repeat until your delivery is polished and unwavering.

Drill 2: Pressure Simulation

Role-play a high-stakes negotiation with a colleague where they introduce last-minute objections. Practice staying calm and handling pushback with conviction.

Drill 3: Play Offense in Sales

In your next sales call, don't wait for the buyer to dictate the next steps. Set the agenda, frame the urgency, and lock in a concrete next action before ending the conversation.

Closing the deal isn't the end of the game, it's the beginning of your next win.

Elite closers know that what happens after the signature is just as important as what led up to it. Your mindset got the deal across the goal line, but how you finish sets the tone for implementation, long-term success, and future revenue.

Finishing strong isn't about checking a box, it's about delivering results, exceeding expectations, and laying the groundwork for referrals, renewals, and expansion.

In the final chapter, we'll break down what it takes to finish with impact, turn new customers into raving fans, and create momentum that carries into your next big win. Let's close this out the right way.

Get access to the Red Zone Selling Resource Center including templates, scripts, and playbooks at redzoneselling.co.

CHAPTER 11

Finishing Strong

Closing Time

Sales, like football, is a game of execution. You can move the ball down the field with great conversations, insightful discovery, and strong presentations, but none of that matters if you don't close. The best sellers, just like the best quarterbacks or elite athletes, understand that winning isn't just about effort; it's about precision, mindset, and making the right plays in the most critical moments.

Everything we've covered in *Red Zone Selling* is designed to help you execute when it counts. To play offense instead of defense. To take control of the deal instead of reacting to the buyer's process. To finish strong instead of letting winnable deals slip away.

Championship athletes and elite sales professionals share one critical trait: mental toughness. They don't let pressure break them; they use it to sharpen their focus. They trust their training, their preparation, and their ability to perform when the game is on the line.

The same applies in sales. Deals will get messy. Buyers will hesitate. Competitors will push back. The sales reps who consistently win aren't the ones who avoid challenges, they're the ones who embrace them.

- When a deal stalls, they find a way to restart momentum.
- When a buyer hesitates, they address concerns head-on.
- When a competitor tries to undercut them, they reinforce value instead of playing defense.

Winning doesn't happen by accident. It happens because you refuse to let obstacles dictate the outcome.

Sales professionals don't lose deals because they lack skill or effort they lose because they fail to execute in the Red Zone. The final stages of a deal are where pressure is highest, stakes are biggest, and hesitation creeps in. This is where elite closers separate themselves:

- They qualify effectively in the Yellow Zone, ensuring they pursue winnable opportunities.
- They build momentum in the Green Zone, keeping deals from stalling.
- They execute with urgency in the Red Zone, ensuring every detail is locked in before closing.

If you control these stages, you control the deal. If you control the deal, you win more often.

No two deals are the same. Just like quarterbacks adjust based on defensive alignment, top sales professionals adapt their approach based on buyer behavior, competition, and timing.

If a deal is dragging, they call an urgency play, anchoring decisions to business impact.

If a stakeholder blocks progress, they call a multi-threading play, engaging new decision-makers.

If a last-minute objection arises, they call an objection-handling play, removing doubt and reinforcing confidence.

Being great at sales isn't about following a rigid script, it's about recognizing the situation and making the right move at the right time.

Reading this book won't make you a top 1% closer, execution will. The strategies, mindset shifts, and tactical plays only work if you implement them. The difference between great salespeople and average ones is simple: Great ones take action.

- They don't wait for buyers to decide, they lead them to a decision.
- They don't hope deals close, they make sure deals close.
- They don't let pressure break them, they thrive in high-stakes moments.

The next time you're in the Red Zone, remember this: The outcome is in your hands. Step up, execute with confidence, and close the deal.

Remember the words of swimming great Michael Phelps: *It's not how you start, it's how you finish.*[8]

Get access to the Red Zone Selling Resource Center including templates, scripts, and playbooks at redzoneselling.co.

---

[8] Phelps has been quoted numerous times in different interviews and in a *Swimmers World* article dated August 15th, 2020, https://www.swimmingworldmagazine.com/news/4-michael-phelps-quotes-to-keep-you-motivated/.

To stay sharp, get updates, and join a network
of elite closers, visit redzoneselling.co and
become part of the Red Zone Selling community.

Author Bio

Vince Beese is a seasoned B2B sales leader with over 25 years of experience driving revenue growth, scaling sales teams, and leading five successful exits. He has generated over $1 billion in revenue, specializing in enterprise sales and go-to-market strategy. Vince is known for building high-performance sales organizations and mentoring sales professionals to exceed their goals.

As the author of *Red Zone Selling*, he shares a structured approach to closing deals with precision. Beyond sales, Vince actively coaches founders, sales leaders, and sales professionals offering insights on closing strategies, win rates, and sales execution.

Passionate about leadership and continuous improvement, Vince thrives on helping others win whether on the field of business or in personal growth. He and his wife Alene have been married for 27 years, and are the parents of three daughters. He resides in Cary, NC.

Get access to the Red Zone Selling Resource Center including templates, scripts, and playbooks at http://redzoneselling.co.

www.ingramcontent.com/pod-product-compliance
Lightning Source LLC
Chambersburg PA
CBHW031133090426
42738CB00008B/1072